TODAY IN DARKEST BRITAIN

Today
in
Darkest Britain

CAUGHEY GAUNTLETT

SALVATIONIST PUBLISHING & SUPPLIES

MARC
Eastbourne

Biblical quotations are from the
New International Version, copyright ©
International Bible Society 1973, 1978, 1984

Front cover photos:
Colour, Tony Stone Photolibrary – London
Black and white, Katalin Arkell – Network Photographers

British Library Cataloguing in Publication Data

Gauntlett, Caughey
    Today in darkest England.
    1. Great Britain. Social conditions – Christian
    viewpoints
    I. Title
    261.83

    ISBN 1–85424–059–5

Salvation Army International Headquarters

101 Queen Victoria Street
London EC4P 4EP

Printed in Great Britain for
MARC, an imprint of Monarch Publications Ltd,
1 St Anne's Road, Eastbourne, E Sussex BN21 3UN by
Richard Clay Ltd, Bungay, Suffolk
Typeset by J&L Composition Ltd, Filey, North Yorkshire

Acknowledgements

My sincere thanks are due to all who have helped in the compilation of this little volume. A number of my colleagues in the Salvation Army, as indicated in the text, have given their time and shared freely their experiences and convictions about the work they are doing. The ring of authenticity, which I hope the reader will discern, is due very largely to their contributions.

Various members of staff at the headquarters of the Army's social and field work have been very helpful in directing my enquiries towards these 'front-line' people. Lt Colonel Margaret White, assistant chief secretary of the Army's Social Services, has organised and co-ordinated the itineraries of my various visits to the different centres, making useful suggestions as to the most valuable places and programmes for my purposes. In addition, her personal knowledge and insights have been quite invaluable in bringing this project to fruition. I accept full responsibility, however, for the views expressed—other than those quoted from named persons—and for the interpretations placed upon events and situations.

To my daughter, Rita, I express grateful appreciation for the laborious, and often thankless, task of typing and repeatedly up-dating the manuscript. Above all, I acknowledge that I could never have set down what follows without the creative and whole-hearted support of my wife, Marjorie. Very much of what I have learned about human problems, particularly from a Christian standpoint, has been from her. Her lifelong interest in, and grasp of, social questions, with their moral and ethical aspects, has been the inspiration for so much of this survey.

Contents

Foreword

In the hundred years that have passed since William Booth pleaded the cause of the 'submerged tenth' in his historic offer of remedial action, *In Darkest England and the Way Out,* society has undergone a many-sided transformation including the changing of social attitudes—for better and for worse.

Yet the centenary of the publication of *In Darkest England* reveals a nation still uneasily aware of division, inequality and deprivation, plus the emergent problems of a permissive, undisciplined and increasingly violent society. There are areas, both geographical and social, where darkest Britain is an appropriate description. In this book Commissioner Caughey Gauntlett, a retired Salvation Army leader, presents the fruits of his personal exploration into these areas. Recalling Booth's book, he describes present-day situations and Salvationists' response, besides calling for action nation-wide to meet the challenge of the 90s.

The Salvation Army recognises that its own human and material resources are pitifully inadequate when faced with the needs its soldiers encounter daily. Thus this book welcomes the efforts of fellow Christians, other bodies, governments and all persons of good-will.

At the same time—and with a century of experience to

confirm the conviction—The Salvation Army affirms that the needs of individuals and society call for more than human resources. The divine factor, saving grace, remains the Salvationist's reliance and hope amid all situations.

It is in that confidence that I offer this book to all who care about the needy in Britain today.

General Eva Burrows

Introduction

Why 'darkest' Britain? Is there any justification for referring to our seemingly 'green and pleasant land' with such a term? What kind of darkness is meant? And what are its causes?

As a nation we are keenly aware of the frightening increase in the number of violent crimes, leading to widespread fear among certain sections of our population. We are regularly presented with horrifying details of drug abuse and sex offences, with the spectre of AIDS lurking menacingly in the background. Child abuse looms large in the daily news, with some appalling revelations of what is happening to innocent children. Yet such is human nature—and perhaps the British temperament in particular—that for many people these dark shadows still seem remote and a little unreal. 'It's terrible, but it hasn't happened in our district, thank God! So it can't be so bad' is quite a common attitude, one which most of us may well have felt at some time or other.

Just 100 years ago, in October 1890, a remarkable book was published in London, with the title *In Darkest England and the Way Out*. The author was William Booth, the founder and self-styled General of the Salvation Army. He had become a prominent figure in Victorian times, variously regarded by his critics as a fanatic, a charlatan and even a swindler. Others were more sympathetic to his sincere but unconventional approach to the task of bringing the gospel to the masses.

He had also earned a considerable reputation for his efforts to ameliorate the misery caused by abject poverty, notably in the East End of London. Seeing the squalor and sheer degradation in which hundreds of thousands lived there, he came to the conclusion that it was pointless to preach to people with empty bellies or cold feet. In his compassionate reaction to all he observed in the course of his preaching ministry, we find the origins of what he was to call the 'social wing' of the Army.

Booth based the first part of his book on a newly published account by the renowned African explorer, Sir Henry M Stanley, of his journeys through what he referred to as 'darkest Africa'. Stanley had been sent by the *New York Herald* to try to find Dr David Livingstone, and his book *Through the Dark Continent* describes his adventure. Stanley's revelation of the conditions in which millions lived there caused quite a sensation. The profound influence and consequences of the slave trade, and practices such as cannibalism and witchcraft, had kept these people at an appallingly low level of existence. Life was cheap, and death often preferable. Any improvement in standards of diet and health, knowledge and spiritual development, were undreamed of. Reflecting upon Stanley's observations, Booth asked, 'As there is a darkest Africa, is there not also a darkest England?'

As he traversed the almost impenetrable forests of central Africa, Stanley noted that his native carriers became 'sodden with despair'. He described their 'brooding sullenness . . . [and] morbid gloom'. The reason was simple, he concluded. The denizens of this vast tropical rain forest had no thought or feeling that the world elsewhere could possibly be anything other than the semi-darkness in which they eked out their existence, as their forebears had done from time immemorial. Life was as it was, and there was no hope of anything different, let alone better.

This journalist-explorer noted two distinct types of pygmy in the region through which he travelled. One was 'a very degraded specimen, with ferret-like eyes, close-set nose, more nearly approaching the baboon than was supposed to be possible—but very human'. The other he described as 'very handsome with frank, open, innocent features ... intelligent ... showing remarkable industry and patience'.

Commenting on this, Booth asked whether so-called civilisation which produces its own barbarians does not also produce its pygmies. Thinking of the very poor of London, whom he had observed at close quarters, he wrote: 'The two tribes of savages, the human baboon and the handsome dwarf ... may be accepted as the two varieties who are continually with us: the vicious, lazy lout, and the toiling slave.' He believed many of them, like the African tribes-people, were devoid of any thought of life becoming other than it was.

In subsequent chapters of his book he went on to write of those brought low through debt, ill-health and the vagaries and injustices of the labour market, as well as by strong drink and the crime which so often stemmed from the abuse of alcohol. 'Drunk for a ha'penny, dead drunk for a penny' was the common condition of thousands who tried thus to escape from the unbearable nature of their circumstances. Women and their young daughters took to the streets. By selling their bodies, they could earn a meagre copper or two to help keep some kind of roof over the family and provide at least a few hunks of bread to stave off starvation.

All this was real, horribly and obscenely real, noted Booth. Deprivation led almost inevitably to degradation, and finally to the welcome oblivion of death. It seemed that there was little basic difference between the fate of the forest-dwellers of Africa and the inhabitants of the slums and gutters of London. Hence Booth's use of the expression 'darkest England'. Hence too his comprehensive scheme, outlined in great detail, as a first step towards providing an escape from the moral morass of the masses who lived in the new conurbations of post-industrial revolution Britain.

Booth wanted to create a sense of hope that life could be different, better. He knew that it was possible, metaphorically speaking, for the sun to shine and so transform the lives of those hitherto restricted to the dank gloom of the 'jungle'. Above all, he passionately believed that God loved each of the poor creatures whom he regularly encountered in at least one part of the otherwise great and glamorous capital of Britain. The British Empire covered vast tracts of the earth's surface (carefully shaded red on the maps of the day!) and generated unprecedented wealth for itself. Yet these riches were so badly distributed that millions literally rotted in squalor while many others lived in great comfort and even luxury. Small wonder that Disraeli, in his novel *Sybil*, described this country as 'two nations': the Privileged and the People. He, of all politicians in the Victorian period, knew this. He had worked long enough to improve the situation, and with some success. The Reform Bill of 1867 was part of the social amelioration brought about under his leadership as Prime Minister.

Booth was quite blunt in his analysis of the social scene with which he and his fellow Salvationists were all too familiar. He provided statistics, backed up by intelligent estimates, to support his challenge to the public authorities, and indeed to the general public. In effect he said, 'This is the true situation—what is to be done about it?'

Writing of 'the lost' of the Victorian era, he referred to 'those who have lost their foothold in society'. These people could not buy their daily bread with the money they earned in a day. They could only obtain the bare minimum of food through vice or crime. He compared the lot of 'the worst criminals in our gaols' favourably with the very poorest 'free' men. He quoted from the historian Thomas Carlyle, who had compared human workers with work horses:

'There are not many horses in England, able and willing to work, which have not due food and lodging, and go about sleek coated, satisfied in heart.'

Booth then asked rhetorically, 'What is the standard towards which we may ... aim with some prospect of realisation in our time?' His reply: 'It is the standard of the London cab-horse'. If it falls, all efforts are directed at getting it onto its feet again—if only to avoid traffic obstruction!' In sum, 'Every cab-horse in London has ... a shelter for the night, food for its stomach, and work allotted to it by which it can earn its corn.' That standard, he concluded, was at that time 'absolutely unattainable by literally millions of our fellow men and women in this country'. He then presented his calculation of the number of people in Britain who lived below that standard.

However, he was no mere observer or scientific analyst. His contemporary and namesake, Charles Booth, had already published some findings on the same conditions in London. These were later extended to seventeen volumes under the title *Life and Labour of the People of London* (Volume 1 was published in 1890). Some of the noted sociologist's observations eventually led to the establishment of a system of state pensions for the elderly. The founder of the Salvation Army was aware of the contents of at least the first volume of the other Booth's work. No doubt these aided him in his efforts to offer practical help to the poor and needy. Essentially a pragmatist, the Salvationist General now outlined carefully constructed plans which he based upon the experience of his colleagues who worked in the most needy areas of the metropolis.

The relatively new movement, first known as the East London Christian Mission, subsequently abbreviated to the Christian Mission, and from 1878 known as the Salvation Army, had already begun to operate in these districts. Those concerned Christians worked among the poorest, the most depraved and sometimes outright criminals. Their ministry of practical Christian caring attracted the attention of both those who supported them and those whose opposition to Booth and his Army often became bitter and acrimonious.

His book, however, substantiated many facts about the society of that time which were virtually unknown to most people in Britain. Only a few of the more enlightened minority suspected even vaguely how widespread the problem was. Booth set out to alert his fellow countrymen to the fact that about ten per cent of the population were living in one form or another of serious deprivation; many were below the sheer poverty line, or the bare subsistence level. He referred to the 'submerged tenth', comprising 'loafers, casuals and criminals, the starving, inmates of workhouses, asylums, prisons and reformatories'. Based on the premise that the incidence of such need was twice as high in London as elsewhere, Booth estimated a national total of some 2,000,000 persons in these categories. To these he added a further 1,000,000 to include those who were dependent upon them—a total of approximately one tenth of the 31,000,000 national population of the day.

It was to this sector of society that Booth felt called as a committed Christian evangelist, and his plans were directed to their needs. He hoped to stir the conscience of the nation, and hopefully to galvanise people to do more than merely wish him well. He needed both moral and financial support, though he stressed that the principle of self-support would be adhered to whenever possible—'No coddling them!' was his brusque instruction to his closest colleagues. While some elements in his comprehensive 'Darkest England' scheme were never brought to fruition, an appreciable part of his vision was realised quickly within the social wing of the Army.

Acknowledgement of the genius behind the whole scheme must be shared between Booth and his remarkable wife, Catherine. Although she was dying of cancer at the time he was evolving his plans, she had had a tremendous influence on the development of his thinking. Theirs was an almost unique partnership.

His faith was rewarded. The book's first edition of 10,000 copies was sold out on the first day. Two further editions, each of 40,000, followed within weeks. A year later a fifth edition was announced, bringing total sales to 200,000! All profits went directly to the scheme. Such national acclaim was in itself evidence of the impact made at the time. As recently as 1970 a paperback reprint was made by Charles Knight & Co Ltd, largely to supply the demand from students and practitioners of sociology, as General Erik Wickberg indicated in his Foreword to this sixth edition.

Our social welfare system in Britain is in considerable measure the outcome of Booth's ideas and ideals. William Beveridge, the architect of the British social security system introduced following the end of World War Two, had much earlier studied Booth's 'Darkest England' scheme. Many of its principles were embodied in the so-called Beveridge Report of 1942—*The Report on Social Insurance and Allied Services*. (More specific reference to this fact will be found at appropriate points in this book.)

In essence Booth proposed to create three types of 'colony', through which would pass such 'submerged' persons as were willing to do an honest day's work for an honest day's pay. In the process, they and their families would have a good chance of escaping from the spiral which tended to drag them down almost relentlessly to the lowest strata of Victorian society.

There was to be a city colony, a farm colony and an overseas colony. The first would be set up in London, and would take the form of several institutions to act as 'harbours of refuge ... in the very centre of the ocean of misery'. The neediest would have their most immediate requirements met: temporary and very basic accommodation, and work within their capacity. He anticipated that a good number of people (mostly men) would then be helped to find more regular paid employment, and so find themselves on the first rung of a ladder by which they could then climb out of the circumstances which had led to their poverty and misery. They would need to show as much will and determination as the Salvationists who were trying to help restore their self-worth and hope.

Many of those entering the city colony, where 'their industry, sincerity and honesty would be tested', would then move on to the farm colony. This was to be established in the provinces (eventually at Hadleigh, Essex), where their physical, moral and spiritual regeneration could be further fostered. A number of these men would possibly move on again at a later stage, this time to a co-operative farm which Booth projected, and which also featured in his scheme.

Finally, a certain number of those who showed appropriate aptitudes, and had an inclination to do so, would be transferred to an agricultural community in one of the new nations of the British Empire, such as South Africa or Canada. Booth had noticed the vast underdeveloped tracts of land in several such countries he had visited in the course of his travels as leader of the rapidly expanding international movement which the Salvation Army had become.

Although he genuinely believed that this third stage of his project would be mutually beneficial to emigrants from the 'old country' and to the recipient lands, he had clearly not anticipated the degree of resistance and even outright opposition it would arouse. Both Australia and New Zealand feared it might lead to a renewal of England's eighteenth-century deportations. If they had only read Booth's plans further, they would have seen how practical and far-seeing he was and would doubtless have been less fearful. Booth confessed to 'great sympathy with those who object to emigration *as carried on hitherto*', adding that he would refuse to have anything to do with compulsory expatriation. He firmly intended that all applicants should be screened as to their suitability and willingness to enter into the venture.

No such overseas colony was in fact established at that time. A little later a number of agricultural schemes were initiated by the Army from within several of the countries in question in which the Army had extended its operations. These were designed chiefly for the training of the young or delinquent—often a combination of the two.

Thus, despite a great deal of personal lobbying by Booth at the highest levels of government in each country which had attracted his attention in this connection, he failed to win their assent. The pressures of those who would have to implement the schemes, and from local workers who feared the loss of their own livelihood, prevailed.

However, the early years of this century saw the development of a variation of this idea, already functioning more sporadically, and which now acted as a partial substitute for the overseas colony. A number of workers had already been helped to emigrate to countries which did not have the problems of overcrowding, unemployment and general urbanisation that were present in Britain. This occurred after Booth had set up an Emigration Advice Bureau in the City of London, around 1904. This gave information to enquirers, forged links with prospective employers overseas, and generally helped to realise the hopes of would-be emigrants. Canada was a primary country of reception for many years, though later the preference shifted to Australia.

Booth's plan to construct a 'salvation ship' for the earlier purpose of establishing his own colonies overseas was transformed into the leasing of existing ocean liners on a charter basis. The programme continued until the outbreak of war in 1939, with a break during the years of World War One. It is of special interest that following the Armistice in 1918, many widows and children of husbands and fathers who had been killed in action were enabled to begin a new life overseas through this agency. Records show that almost

250,000 people were helped to emigrate during the four decades or so of this operation.

This was no mere substitute for the more ambitious colonisation plan. Booth had additionally foreseen emigration as a means of helping those better prepared than the down-and-outs to establish the new colonies and relieve the over-population and unemployment in Britain. As always in this great-heart's proposals, Salvationists were on hand at the ports of embarkation, on the ships, and at the points of arrival, to ensure the smoothest possible resettlement of such people. Booth felt that this extra touch was essential to any scheme designed to uplift, transform and stabilise those whose lives had been blighted or stunted by their former surroundings.

At this point some reference must be made to the way in which William Booth's attitude towards practical social involvement as part of his evangelistic motivation gradually changed. From his early youth he had felt impelled to preach the gospel, mainly in the more conventional sense. He was already widely known as a passionate preacher. It was only with the passing of the years that he came to acknowledge and accept that he must help respond to the physical and material needs of those deprived of even the most basic necessities, if he hoped to save their souls. Yet spiritual motivation remained the basis of his efforts in this direction.

He was surely aware of such verses as those in the Epistle of James concerning 'faith without works', though he was naturally unaware of the contemporary ring of some of the more recently published translations and paraphrases. In chapter 2, verses 14–17, the apostle asks:

> Dear brothers, what's the use of saying that you have faith and are Christians if you aren't proving it by helping others? Will *that* kind of faith save anyone? If you have a friend who is in need of food and clothing, and you say to him, 'Well, good-bye and God bless you; stay warm and eat up,' and then don't give him clothes or food, what good does that do? ... Faith that

doesn't show itself by good works . . . is dead and useless (The Living Bible).

In 1910, at the age of eighty-one, Booth was questioned on this very subject by a reporter. He replied that it was only partly true that the rehabilitation of religion in Britain would come along the line of social service: 'It is only when we get more soul into our lives that we are able to do any good . . . all the social activity of the Army is the outcome of the spiritual life of its members.' Eighty years on, this is still the fundamental motivation of all such work carried out by Salvationists and their fellow workers.

As recently as 1978, Lt Colonel George Carpenter, a retired Australian Salvation Army officer, concluded a lecture to the movement's international social conference in London with these words: 'The day of the big, expensive, organised social work may be declining. I believe the day of the kindly, thoughtful, generous, non-professional caring ministry of the ordinary salvationist is about to dawn.'

Carpenter refers to the possibility of a highly structured social programme being 'liquidated overnight by decree'—a reference to unsympathetic government action in certain countries. He states that 'a Spirit-filled, spontaneous, neighbourhood ministry by the Salvationist/Christian is virtually indestructible'.

It was sheer Christian compassion which led Booth and his colleagues to do something practical for the neediest, in God's name. No developed theology of Christian social service evolved at the time—they were far too busy getting on with the job. Even today, when there is a growing number of university educated Salvation Army officers and others engaged in such programmes, there is still no 'official' doctrine on the subject. 'Thou shalt love the Lord thy God . . . and thy neighbour as thyself' remains the guiding principle of Salvationists all around the world. Their remedial and rehabilitation work is still seen as redemptive, with the prayer that spiritual regeneration will come to at least some of those so helped. Every effort is made to offer spiritual counsel, without 'ramming religion down people's throats'. The aim is to help people to find a solution to their problems in a personal experience of salvation in Christ.

Thus 'preaching the good news to the poor' comes at the head of the list of biblically-based objectives in the Army's social operations. To 'heal the broken-hearted' and 'preach deliverance to the captives'; to 'set at liberty those who are oppressed' and 'comfort those who mourn' is justification enough for all engaged in this work.

At times there has been a wide divergence of opinion and conviction, sometimes flaring into acrimonious dispute, between those Christians who adhere to a fundamentalist insistence upon purely spiritual priorities and those who hold that the gospel of Jesus Christ inevitably has a strong 'social' element in it.

Suffice it to say here that the publication in 1890 of *In Darkest England* marked the culmination of a growing certainty in the mind of its author that the hungry must be fed, the naked clothed and the sick healed as an inescapable part of the responsibility of Christ's servants. In no other way can the fact of God's love for all, and especially the downtrodden and under-privileged, be communicated effectively and redemptively.

This present volume therefore has two aims. First, to alert the British public of the 1990s to some of the more serious aspects of poverty, deprivation and, in many cases, degradation in this country. Secondly, to give some account of what William Booth's successors are attempting in our own times, by way of meeting human need in those circumstances. The reader will note that, like their founder, Salvationists today work unashamedly in the name and Spirit of Jesus Christ. They believe that the spiritual dimension is essential in undertaking such a task and in helping those concerned to find their way out of the 'darkness'. Increasingly such social enterprises have to be undertaken in collaboration with other societies and associations based on Christian principles. Close co-operation with both local and central government and statutory bodies is also necessary—though never where compromise of such basic precepts and principles would be involved.

Clearly, enormous progress has been made in social welfare provisions in Britain since the Victorian and Edwardian periods. Standards have risen out of all proportion to the highest hopes of folk like Booth. And with that upward trend general expectations have also increased. Despite the overtly materialistic and secular ethos which this development has produced, it is increasingly recognised today that economic and material measures in themselves are inadequate to bring about the redemption of the whole person.

Some of the root causes of suffering and misery which Booth and others pointed out a century ago, remain today, and are widely acknowledged as such by most people. To the evils of alcohol abuse must be added the appalling consequences of addictive drug consumption, sexual promiscuity and perversion, and the pornography industry. The apparently harmless 'profit motive' in business and commerce—some would call it vital for national prosperity —is now seen to lead all too often to sheer greed, ruthless exploitation and widespread corruption. The recent spate of major financial scandals in London and elsewhere is only the tip of the iceberg in this respect.

Administrative and legislative devices designed to act as checks and balances, necessary though they undoubtedly are, will inevitably have only limited effect. Until the nature of man is radically altered and redeemed, morally dubious and often criminal practices will continue to spread like a cancer in society. The upshot can only be an ongoing erosion of ethical standards and values, and an accelerating breakdown of the moral fibre of society itself.

The social and spiritual malaise of Britain today cannot be adequately dealt with by government or private agencies alone. Collaboration is vital. The disinterested work of legislators, administrators and professional social practitioners will always require the moral and spiritual influence evidenced in the programmes of Christian and other welfare organisations. The religious and moral motivation of many charitable welfare bodies will certainly continue to be a key element in aiding those caught in the network of evil factors which reduce so many to an almost sub-human existence—even today.

A summary of matters for concern to the Salvation Army is given at the end of this book. It is not simply a lone voice, but includes some of the recent social and moral challenges from others. From the Army's point of view, these issues are based on the experience, observations and convictions of many Salvationists in this country. Their labour of love is supported by countless other Christians and those with a strong humanitarian conscience. It is our hope and prayer that the publication of this book may help to hasten the day when more just structures come into being, in which divine redemption can operate freely among the people of this land, reflecting the glory of God's purposes for mankind.

I

How the Work Grew

Before turning to a closer consideration of British society today, and the current work of the Salvation Army, we should perhaps ask what became of Booth's great vision. To what extent was his comprehensive and ambitious scheme put into practice? How far did it succeed in its aims to alleviate the lot of the poor and downtrodden of his day? What has been the ongoing result of his appeal to the conscience of the nation at that time, following its tremendous initial impact?

Reference has already been made to some parts of the 'Darkest England' programme which remained unfulfilled, particularly the overseas agricultural colonies. We have noted that both understandable concern and vested interests prevented the realisation of Booth's hopes and plans in that direction.

William (later, Lord) Beveridge has already been mentioned as the architect of this country's present-day social welfare system. In fact, he had a lifelong concern for social reform, and had early in life established quite a reputation for himself as an authority on unemployment. His study, *Unemployment—a Problem of Industry*, had made him known before Winston Churchill, as President of the Board of Trade, brought him into that government department in 1908.

Beveridge was soon engaged in preparing draft legislation

on the subject, for presentation to parliament. The enabling Act was approved in 1909, and the first eighty-three labour exchanges opened their doors in February of the following year. That was almost twenty years after William Booth's first venture into that particular field; he had established such an office in Upper Thames Street in the City of London in June 1890. In the first seven years, more than 80,000 men had registered there, and almost 70,000 had secured employment. The numbers virtually doubled in the next five years.

Of much wider interest, however, are Beveridge's observations on the whole of the 'Darkest England' scheme. These were recorded around 1910, and subsequently incorporated in a symposium on the life and work of William Booth, published sometime between then and 1912. With the title *The Social Work of The Salvation Army*, this document is the only comprehensive and independent analysis and evaluation of the situation, two decades after the launching of Booth's project. It is clearly the result of wide-ranging enquiry and careful research, and provides some idea as to how far the dream of 1890 had been realised within twenty years.

Outlining Booth's original proposals, Beveridge refers to 'this scheme of social regeneration obviously right in its main principles; a scheme hopeful yet practical'. In reply to the question, 'How has it been realised?' he noted that the city and farm colonies had already become well established, while the overseas colony 'still remains a dream'. Quite clearly a great deal had been accomplished for vagrant men and also men involved in crime, at least by way of providing accommodation, food and clothing. Several thousand had also found work, through centres in a number of major cities outside London, in addition to the main work in the capital itself.

However, he went on to state, 'The problems which the 'Darkest England' scheme was to solve appear at present to be as far off a solution as ever, in spite of all the efforts of the Salvation Army, the Church Army and countless other organisations. The morass of squalor shows no visible dent.' A sobering comment, which also underlines the fact that others were working towards the same end that Booth had in mind, though probably on a smaller scale.

The report continues: 'The shelters of the Salvation Army and other organisations are always full,' but adds that the number of 'houseless' is probably greater than before.

Beveridge then poses the more penetrating question: 'How far has [it] proved regenerative?' He cannot have missed Booth's reiterated emphasis upon this aspect of his scheme. In all fairness he limits the significance of the question to 'those coming under its [the Army's] influence', rather than 'the whole of the army of the outcast'.

He concluded that the answer must be different for the two sides of the Army's social work—the men's and women's. In a number of homes in London, girls and young women were 'received, set to work and trained'. Adequate staff, longer-term care and training and relatively small numbers of residents helped to ensure that good character was formed. The process could quite justifiably be termed 'regenerative'. Work was quite easily found for those trainees, and follow-up was assured for at least five years. Visits and correspondence were the responsibility of one designated officer on the staff of each centre.

Quoting some quite astonishing statistics relating to this after-care, Beveridge writes of 'an excellent piece of work, in full accord with the spirit of the "Darkest England" proposals'. He is quite persuaded that the Army 'catches up many who are lost or in danger of being lost, and makes them useful members of society'.

In contrast, the work among men 'presents a curiously different picture'. Allowing that individuals are sometimes 'restored from crime and vice and squalor to independence and self respect', the 'merely weak-willed and broken in spirit' do not seem to have been 'rescued' at all. Beveridge advanced several possible reasons for this, any one or more of which might apply. The numbers of men in such centres are very much larger than in those for women. Consequently 'the possibility of sustained individual influence is correspondingly less, or non-existent'. There is little or no reliable information as to what happened to such men while being assisted materially.

At best, only a small number of men entering the 're-generative' centres were permanently aided. There was a high rate of turnover of residents in the city colony, many failing to acquire sufficient orderliness to make use of the help available.

Beveridge, nothing if not perceptive in his observations, feared that all too many men who, the Salvationists claimed, had been 'helpfully influenced' might simply be slipping back into the abyss.

Lt Colonel George Carpenter (R) has made a considerable study of the impact of Booth's great project at the time, and of the various reactions to it. He summarised Beveridge's reactions as follows:

> He is not sparing in his criticism of some aspects of the scheme, which had been operating for almost twenty years, but he concludes with an important acknowledgement. 'The religious enthusiasm of the Salvation Army gives it one of the great qualifications for success. It should not be impossible to engraft thereon the other great qualification, the spirit of knowledge and self-criticism.'

At this point Beveridge fully aligns himself with Booth's basic criteria for the whole plan. Those same principles have directed and motivated all Salvationist programmes of a practical nature. 'Unless there be a change in the whole man as well as in his surroundings, no dealing with the outcast can be of any avail.' If the individual is merely helped from day to day, 'you would probably increase the evil with which you are attempting to deal' was the Army founder's dictum. 'You had much better let the whole thing alone,' he added.

A further crucial question which Beveridge then addressed was whether those working with such unwieldy numbers of men 'really accepted the difficult standards, and expressed the lofty ideals set up by General Booth'.

As mentioned earlier, this comprehensive assessment and critique was almost unique in circles outside the movement, and as such it has particular significance. However, the London *Times* made its own evaluation of Booth's work, also in 1910. In the course of a lengthy article, the writer noted:

> The comparative paucity of completely satisfactory results means that the 'Darkest England' scheme was, as such, impracticable. It was too sanguine; the task which Booth set himself was superhuman. He probably sees that himself in looking back after the lapse of twenty-one years. But that does not make his work a failure. On the contrary it is an amazing, one may even say a stupendous, success. . . . To have built up this world-wide organisation . . . engaged in active, helping human work, holding out a hand to those who need it . . . and to have done this through the power and on the basis of a pure, Christian enthusiasm in these latter days of materialistic and rationalistic domination—such an achievement can only be called great.

Booth himself, however, was a supreme pragmatist. He was more than willing to be strongly self-critical—and that proved uncomfortable for some of those working under his direction. Yet he saw both sides of the equation, and intended to present a balanced view of the whole project. Addressing officers in a council meeting he said, 'True, we have not yet [1896] done everything promised at the outset. But we have, I think, amply made up by doing some things not named.' Later (1906), he made known that some dozen or more new branches of work had been added to the scheme. In addition to such evocative forms as 'farthing breakfasts for children', 'midnight soup kitchens' and 'midnight work amongst women', are found some rather more puzzling expressions of his desire to help various categories of needy folk. For what (regenerative) purpose 'shoe-blacking brigades' were established must be left to the reader's imagination. No doubt his 'street-cleaning brigades' helped remove some of the filthy refuse which, we are told, littered the streets of London almost permanently in those days. Improved public hygiene was no doubt in his mind, and, then as now, the idea of involving people otherwise unemployed in community projects can be mutually beneficial. We would like to believe that some character building resulted from this work, with improved motivation in some, at least.

At much the same time, this remarkable man referred to the many facets of his original proposals. Out of twenty-nine, only eight had not been established seventeen years later. These included a 'travelling hospital', 'refuges for street children' and 'asylums for moral lunatics'. Such expressions have a curiously contemporary ring to them!

Major Jenty Fairbank, director of the Army's international heritage centre in London, has collated much information concerning that period from a variety of sources. Her book, *Booth's Boots*, gives fascinating insights into the way in which Booth's mind and spirit turned restlessly and relentlessly to the many forms of human need and suffering he encountered. She writes: 'Not that Booth's spectacles were rose-tinted. His eagle eye quickly marked any deficiency, and his tongue was not slow in pointing it out.' In 1911, she records, he addressed Salvation Army officer delegates at an international social council. By way of admonition he declared: 'In the history of the social work . . . there have been, as you know, any number of shortcomings. We have not realised all our expectations nor fulfilled all our dreams.'

He clearly indicated that this was to be expected—an imperfect organisation staffed by imperfect people in an imperfect world naturally produced imperfect results. But he continued with what were certainly unpalatable truths for some present:

> There has been a great lack of direct aim at the true goal of our social work on the part of some officers who have been engaged in its direction. Some of us have been content with a 'soup-and-blanket' regime. Our social work is essentially a religious business. Only with pity, love and the power of the Holy Ghost can there be any great success.

Even more bluntly, he refers to 'the lamentable fact that some of our officers have been deficient in personal religion'. His earlier comment that 'you get out of a thing only as much as you put in' must apply particularly to the example and spiritual influence of those ministering in God's name. Ezekiel's warning to the shepherds who feed themselves rather than feeding the flock (Ezek 34:2) is timeless in its application. Or Paul's reference to the need for self-discipline in a spiritual ministry 'so that after I have preached to others, I myself will not be disqualified' (1 Cor 9:27).

Shortage of suitable staff was being dealt with by a programme of training—something which was less axiomatic then than nowadays. There was the ongoing need for funding too. But despite the problems and setbacks Booth, at eighty-two, was optimistic: 'Nevertheless, and notwithstanding all our shortcomings, the position now occupied by our social operations, and their influence . . . is in evidence . . . on every hand.'

Thus there is no great difference between Booth's and Beveridge's thoughts at that point. The latter saw the scheme from the vantage point of an objective observer. He was able to research and evaluate statistics and other data without being directly involved. The former, obviously conscious of the day-to-day struggles to come to grips with what Beveridge referred to as the Army's 'nearly hopeless task', felt that history would vindicate his bold venture.

'Truly, our future chroniclers will have to record the fact that our social operations imparted a divine dignity' to those struggles. Booth was clear that some of his colleagues had lost sight of his primary aims. He might nevertheless have felt that Beveridge was exaggerating somewhat when he wrote that 'in spite of every effort, the saving of the soul has been driven into the background'. Even then, he very reasonably added that his view 'survives the fullest appreciation of the devotion and the splendid hopefulness' of those engaged in this compassionate endeavour.

Such devotion and hopefulness still characterise the work today, a century on from the inception of the 'Darkest England' programme, both in Britain and in more than eighty countries around the world. Such work is, by its very nature, never easy, and success is often impossible to judge. Yet the spirit in which it is done imparts its own 'divine dignity'.

Yet some Christians still ask: 'Should the church become involved in such charitable work?' There are those who would reply in the negative, though it is now widely accepted that the church, as the body of Christ, would be failing in its mission if its members turned away from their fellows in material need. Christ's parable about the Good Samaritan has entered into the life and language of our nation to the point where anyone doing a good turn for someone else might earn that epithet. The name 'Samaritans' is almost universally associated with, and respected as, a caring agency providing a life-line for desperate people.

There is one last point to the question of Christian social service which merits attention. It combines both the philosophy and policy of such work. Have residential institutions outlived their usefulness? After all, the man of Samaria did not found a refuge for victims of highway robbery, neither in Jerusalem nor in Jericho. He simply did what he could, as an individual, using available facilities—the local inn, in that story. The words 'solidarity' and 'mutual responsibility' so casually bandied about in these days, really express this spirit.

Mrs Elizabeth Cottrill, a very ordinary resident of Whitechapel, London, in the second half of the nineteenth century, took into her own home some of the young girls she encountered in the neighbourhood. They had been living in (some doubtless even sold into) prostitution and wanted to escape. She became their good Samaritan. Her home became 'the gateway to heaven' for some of those young women who had unwittingly become enslaved in an evil and darkened way of life. That ministry began, almost unrecorded at the time in the 1870s, and her name is now linked with the very beginnings of Salvation Army social work.

From that simple act of compassion and caring there developed a network of rescue and redemptive centres which at their peak housed several thousand people every day of the year in this century. Yet in professional sociological circles today, many are thinking about alternatives. For instance, government policy has turned more and more from the idea of children's homes to that of fostering. Many who are mentally ill are being released into the community from the institutions which have been home to them for decades, in some instances. Without great care, this could become no more than a euphemism for turning such people loose, unprotected and left to fend for themselves—something they are often quite unable to do.

Some social welfare authorities are critical of Christian agencies which 'bring religion into their work'. Others are opposed—perhaps with some measure of arguable justification—to the maintenance of large hostels, in particular. In some instances they insist that these be phased out. The possibility of institutional social operations being terminated, or taken over by secular authorities, cannot be excluded. How then would the vital Christian ingredient in this type of work be maintained?

It is one purpose of this book to show what both the residential (institutional) and community-based programmes operated by Salvationists, individually and as a movement, are achieving. The background will inevitably be the society of which we are all a part, but aspects of which are unknown—or ignored—by many. The motivation will be seen to be the love and the power of God—today as a hundred years ago.

2

The Poor—Always with You

It's the rich what gets the pleasure,
It's the poor what gets the blame;
It's the same the 'ole world over—
Isn't it a ★ ★ ★ shame!

So runs an old Cockney music-hall ditty which, like many another of its kind, expresses one of life's abiding truths in simple, stark terms. It may have contained an element of *double entendre* with sexual overtones, but the last line (with whatever adjective may be used) is in fact a gross understatement. Real poverty existing side by side with great wealth, is a moral condemnation upon society. The abuse or exploitation—even the apathetic neglect—of the poor by those with greater material substance is intolerable in any truly civilised community, especially a Christian one.

Yet it has never really been any different. Revolutions, usually intended to create a more egalitarian and fundamentally just society, have enjoyed at best a limited measure of success. And where people have become more equal, or society somewhat more even-handed, it has often not lasted for long. Without a basic regeneration of human nature some will always acquire power over others and use it shamelessly for their own ends. Some will benefit through hard work, using their natural abilities to develop themselves and further their interests, while others appear to be incapable of doing so—for whatever reason. Laws will be enacted to ensure the same benefits for all, only for a segment of society to ignore or flout them. So poverty persists. The poor seem always to be with us.

Within church history, perhaps most notably in Method-ism, people have enhanced their social skills and raised their material standard of living once they became converted. John Wesley exhorted his followers to 'earn all you can, save all you can and give all you can'. His 'Rule of Conduct' included the following:

> Do all the good you can, by all the means you can;
> In all the ways you can, in all the places you can;
> To all the people you can, as long as you can.

Many committed Christians, whose spiritual rebirth and newly-found faith have led to a radical transformation of their lifestyle, have discovered the economic and material benefits of sobriety and frugality. Salvationists and others who trace their spiritual heritage to Methodism are among these, with the emphasis firmly on the principle of giving and doing good (though without becoming 'do-gooders' in the conventional sense).

The various branches of Protestantism have evolved dif-fering priorities in this respect. Some have insisted that the church should concern itself solely with spiritual matters, while others have fastened upon Jesus' teaching about love for God being expressed in love for their fellows. The great Scottish reformer, John Knox, included in his *Book of Discipline* the teaching that in every parish those unable to work should be supported out of public funds. (He also declared that those able to work should be compelled to do so!) The Catholic tradition, translated into practical forms of charitable work, is of such long standing as to predate the endeavours of other Christian disciplines.

Wesley succeeded to some extent in changing the thinking of the middle classes of his day in England in favour of industry and sobriety. He also taught that wealth should be considered as a trust. Quite apart from the officially sponsored programmes of the churches, society has been enormously enriched and enlightened by the charitable and philanthropic institutions established by individual social reformers. Names such as Shaftesbury, Howard, Wilberforce, Barnado and Nightingale are representative of many others who have approached the fundamental problems of poverty and injustice with an inner spiritual conviction born of their personal faith. Their quickened awareness of the nature of God, and of the consequent responsibility of all who seek truly to help bring about his 'will on earth, as in heaven', has been a strongly determinative factor in the growth of the modern social welfare programme. Yet today we hear repeated comments from certain political quarters in Britain, suggesting that the churches should not meddle in politics, when Christians challenge the government to alleviate deprivation and misery. The reaction to *Faith in the City* (Church House Publishing), the 1985 report of the Archbishop of Canterbury's Commission on Urban Priority Areas, was an example of this.

Much Christian teaching of earlier days has been overtaken by the rapid social and legislative changes in this country over the past half century. The concept of the welfare state has enveloped and at the same time largely secularised such emphases. Commenting on this, George Carpenter says that the social welfare services which developed from Beveridge's studies 'grew up in a secular humanist society and developed their own ethos. Less is heard of religious enthusiasm and more of knowledge. What is more, with the complete secularisation of social studies, "religious enthusiasm" has come to be seen as inappropriate.'

Social welfare has become a mainly political issue as to how far caring and sharing should go. Government will decide who should benefit, and to what extent, because government pays. But with whose money does it pay? The clash of political ideologies has all but eliminated the religious motivation which arises from an individual's consciousness of his responsibilities towards his fellow men before God. Wealth is the target of the Chancellor's taxation policies, and the notion that it has been given by God to be held in trust has been largely lost.

The nature of poverty is currently being discussed publicly, and that is no bad thing. Comments on the subject made by John Moore, then Social Security Secretary, have given rise to passionate debate. It is true, as the *War Cry* (3rd June, 1989) comments, that 'the desperate, disease-ridden conditions of the slums of a hundred years ago' have largely disappeared. A sense of proportion is needed. Yet the same commentary also notes that 'some other government ministers have managed to give the impression that they don't actually understand the social problems they are dealing with'. The *War Cry* adds that 'it hardly helped John Moore's case when comparisons were made between his mansion and the dwellings of the people he is assigned to help'. The ethical concern over grossly unequal distribution of wealth is still all too often overlooked nowadays.

That was certainly not the case with William Booth, however. He and his soul-partner, Catherine, must be counted among the most effective and successful social reformers of modern times. As already mentioned, they spent their lives in desperate efforts to ameliorate the plight of the poor and those who had become the victims of the many off-shoots of poverty: crime, disease, homelessness and hopelessness. (William Beveridge identified 'five giants in the path of social progress: want, disease, ignorance, squalor and idleness'.) The enduring significance of their work was subsequently acknowledged not only by Beveridge, but also by a leading British social historian. In his best-known work, *English Social History* (1932), Professor G M Trevelyan wrote: 'The Salvation Army, founded by General Booth, brought the enthusiasm of conversion, after Wesley's original fashion, to the army of the home-less and unfed, to the drunkard, the criminal and the harlot.'

This erstwhile Regius Professor of History at Cambridge University went on:

It was significant that the Salvation Army regarded social work and care for the material conditions of the poor and outcast as being an essential part of the Christian mission to the souls of men and women. It was largely for this reason that its power has become a permanent feature of modern English life.

A quite different observer of the Victorian scene was the noted poet, Francis Thompson. Addicted to opium, he saw life 'from the bottom up', having been destitute for some years. During this period he spent some time in one of the Army's London hostels. His best-known poem, 'The Hound of Heaven', describes God lovingly pursuing the human soul through all its devious experiences. Some years later Thompson wrote: 'I have knowledge more intimate than most men's of this life which is not a life . . . in which men rob and women vend themselves.' In London he had seen that 'misery cries out . . . from the kerbstone, despair passes me by in the ways'.

Having read Booth's *Darkest England and the Way Out*, 'put forward by a singular personality', he commented that 'here is at last a man who has formulated a comprehensive scheme, and has dared to take upon himself its execution . . . in God's name, give him the contract!'[1] He clearly knew better than most British people of that day how great the need was for such a plan.

Among Booth's admirers and supporters was Beatrice Webb. She and her husband, Sidney, wrote of him as 'the determined opponent' of an 'alliance between a discriminat-ing philanthropy and a deterrent Poor Law'. This, they stated, left hundreds of thousands of people outside the scope of such a combination of selective do-gooding and detested legislation. (The provisions of the Poor Law included the dreaded workhouse; the use of the word 'pauper' also stemmed from this source.) They added that the destitution of such masses was real enough to constitute a social danger.

A basic principle of socialism is co-operation rather than competition. Of course, there are times when the stimulus of competition is essential—but not when people's personal dignity and well-being are threatened by poverty. The efforts of the Salvation Army's founder, and others like him, depended to a large extent upon co-operation in two main ways. It required a working together of the church and the public authorities; but even more, a close and dependent co-operation between man and God. St Paul used the expression, 'fellow workers' (2 Cor 6:1), variously rendered in contemporary translations and paraphrases as 'partners', 'collaborators' and 'fellow workers' with God.

Booth's personal convictions about this co-operation gave him confidence that what he had begun would be continued by others. In London's Royal Albert Hall, the half-blind eighty-three-year-old gave his last public address. His words on that occasion have almost become a motto for those Salvationists who have engaged in helping poor people of so many kinds since then:

> While women weep as they do now—I'll fight;
> While little children go hungry as they do now—I'll fight;
> While men go to prison, in and out, in and out, as they do now—I'll fight;
> While there is a drunkard left, while there is a poor lost girl upon the streets—I'll fight!;
> While there remains one dark soul without the light of God, I'll fight—I'll fight to the very end!

On that spring day in 1912, his fighting days were virtually over. The weeks which followed brought eye surgery which weakened the old warrior's hold on life.

Within a hundred days he had 'laid down his sword', as the announcement had it. Hours beforehand, he had pressed his son and designated successor, Bramwell, to 'do more for the homeless of the world'. The old fire and wit flickered momentarily in him as he added in response to Bramwell's promise to do so, 'Mind, if you don't I shall come back and haunt you!'

Most Salvationists since then would probably have anticipated some such visitation had they failed in the task which each soldier (member) of the Army accepts when being 'sworn in': 'Feeling that the love of Christ, who died to save me, requires from me this devotion of my life to his service for the salvation of the world ... of my own free will ... I enter into this undertaking.'

Booth's followers and successors were not the only people who have felt impelled by their love for God to serve him by caring for the poor and outcast. Many friends have allied themselves to this work and helped further the cause. One such was Hugh Redwood, a Bristolian working as a Fleet Street journalist in London. His responsibility as night editor of a national daily newspaper brought him into direct contact with Salvationists who were on the spot with relief when the River Thames overflowed its banks in London's West End in January 1928. Inevitably it was the poor who suffered, and the efficient navy-blue uniformed 'servants of all' were there to rescue folk from their flooded basement dwellings. They naturally worked alongside the public emergency services, but on hand-carts and horse-drawn wagons they brought food and hot drinks, blankets and clothing for those who could safely be left. Others were taken to places of safety, together with a few precious belongings. These were the Army's slum officers.

As far back as 1884, William Booth had established centres in some of the worst slum areas of London. A pamphlet had been published by a church minister, revealing some of the appalling conditions in such districts. In an article printed in the *War Cry*, Booth had made reference to this, adding that the information had undoubtedly shocked 'those who have hitherto been too busy, or too lazy . . . at ease . . . respectable . . . or pious to go amongst the outcast classes to try and save them'. But there was nothing new there for the 'salvationist who has to face [their] violence and brutality every night of his life'.

Thus a system of direct, practical aid for such people came into being, with the quite literal name of 'cellar, gutter and garret brigades'. Rooms were taken in several of the capital's most deprived areas, and young women officer-cadets were assigned to visit from house to house. They were to determine the specific needs, and go on to meet them. Scrubbing out filthy houses, washing incredibly dirty children (and, on occasion, adults), nursing the sick and comforting the dying or disconsolate. All this and more was to become part of their everyday lives in this sub-stratum of British society.

The work soon spread to other cities. The need was increasingly revealed to be greater and deeper than almost anyone had imagined. And it was from several such inner-London slum posts that the emergency relief team had assembled in and around Westminster on that fateful night early in 1928. Hugh Redwood the journalist stumbled inadvertently across a story which was to lead to a radical change in his own life. It would also herald a change of name for such Salvationist samaritan centres. The man from Fleet Street, who came to be known as the 'big brother' of these dedicated women, henceforth devoted much of his time, energies and money both in writing about the League of Goodwill work, and in engaging himself personally whenever possible. His best-known book, *God in the Slums*, published in 1930, was followed by others which challenged Christians as to their response to the appalling poverty in their midst.

Though never officially a part of the 'Darkest England'

scheme, the newly designated Goodwill League operated in exactly the same spirit as the city colonies and other extensions of Booth's project. Goodwill centres still operate today in some thirty places within the United Kingdom. With certain necessary adaptations, they still work along the lines of the cellar, gutter and garret brigades and the slum posts. (An old Cockney phrase would call this 'same meat, different gravy'!) They provide help for the underprivileged and thus bring at least some ray of light and hope into otherwise darkened lives—today, in 'darkest' Britain. Their story will feature in Chapter 9.

But now we face again the question as to what is implied by the alleged 'darkness' in our nation, a hundred years on from the launching of the visionary 'Darkest England' scheme. By contrast with the East End of London a century ago, today's inner-urban situation has greatly improved. That is not to say that there is no poverty or deprivation, squalor or misery now. It is all too obvious that several hundreds of thousands of our fellow citizens living in the larger conurbations experience continuing distress and despair. Indeed, it is not only in the so-called 'urban priority areas' that such poverty exists; in thinly veiled form it may be found almost anywhere.

Expectations have greatly increased in recent years. The creation of the social welfare systems in the period following World War Two has largely contributed to this improvement in living standards and to a parallel raising of hopes. Indeed, there is currently much talk about the 'rights' of the underprivileged—something unheard of in Victorian England. Those who were referred to then as 'the masses' are now 'the public'—a significant change!

Overall, public hygiene has vastly improved, however undesirable conditions may be in a minority of districts. The provision of sewerage and drainage, plumbing installations and general household amenities, together with certain standards in housing construction (despite some notable exceptions) has improved living conditions very considerably. That fact will recur in the pages of this book, as we consider the changing forms of deprivation and need, and consequently of remedies. Yet despite this, the thought often springs almost instinctively to mind: fundamentally, much remains unchanged.

The sheer squalor of those days has largely gone. However, there are many very poor people today who feel that they are being 'ground into the dust' through lack of what are considered 'basics of life' in the twentieth century. In that sense, 'grinding' poverty has not yet disappeared by any means. Various benefits are available for many categories of disadvantaged people, such as even far-seeing folk in Victorian times could hardly have envisaged. But there are some glaring gaps in the system. In 1989 child benefit was frozen for the second successive year, despite unexpectedly high inflation. For the unemployed in areas with little prospect of alternative work for a long time, life is proving to be very hard. Youngsters of sixteen and seventeen are almost written off if they have no work and are no longer living at home. And there are many such, as this record will show. Many an older person, especially if living alone, is hard pressed to manage, despite certain supplementary benefits. Media reports have highlighted this dilemma, with accounts of elderly people found suffering from hypothermia because they could not afford to use more gas or electricity. A considerable number of such people regard their last few hundred pounds of savings as being sacrosanct —'for my funeral'—and choose to freeze rather than dip into that final bastion of their self-respect. They are quite often aware that the question of paying for their burial would create family feuding if no sum were in reserve.

These are just some of the groups whose needs and relative hardship are very real. If the situation appears much less dramatic than the conditions in which millions barely survived a hundred years ago, the anguish, despair and feelings of hopelessness and rejection are no less real than they were in that earlier period.

A continuing polarisation is taking place in our society. The better-off are becoming even more prosperous while the plight of the worse-off is deteriorating. A recent report in *The Times* business supplement blandly recorded that 'the average household is £7 a week better off as a result of the tax and benefit changes made during the Thatcher decade'. The same report, however, conceded that 'richer households have benefited more than poorer ones and some people, such as the single unemployed, have lost out'.

It is undeniable that certain changes have worked to the relative advantage of some of the less well-off. One aspect of these changes—which appear to be introduced with bewildering frequency and complexity—is that many people who are entitled to some form of benefit do not claim it. Whether this is due to the feeling of some older people that such benefits are a form of charity, which the culture of their early years rejected, or whether those who miss out do so for lack of clear information, is difficult to determine. Yet the effects are real enough.

The Times report just referred to was based on a research document, *Taxation and Social Security 1979–1989: The Impact on Household Incomes* (Paul Johnson & Graham Stark—Institute for Fiscal Studies). It contains the following statement, which fully confirms the relevance of the verse quoted at the head of this chapter: 'Half the total give-away has gone to the richest ten per cent, while the poorest third of households have gained only £1.30 a week.' (Clearly the sums quoted are adjusted to take account of inflation and represent spending power.)

By contrast, it is reported: 'Family credit has benefited lower-earning working couples with children, but better-off couples have suffered from the cut in the real value of child benefit.'

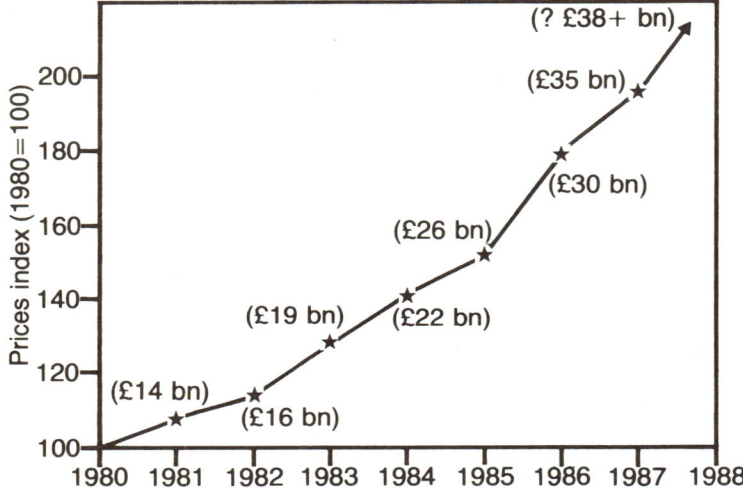

UK — Total consumer credit (excluding house purchase)

The gap between the 'haves' and the 'have nots' in British society is widening, as indeed it is among the nations of the world. And between the two groupings there is emerging another, recently referred to as the 'have-not-yets'. These are the hopeful folk, striving for something better than they have known. Thus it appears that the struggles of very many for economic survival, at a level which allows for a minimum of human dignity, continue. And that struggle will go on as long as government policies are focused so narrowly upon the operation of market forces, and public attitudes are centred on economic prosperity. This is all a far cry from notions of solidarity, of 'loving my neighbour as myself'. Nor is much change to be expected until there is a swing away from the present strong emphasis on material values to much stronger ethical and spiritual considerations.

From the foregoing it is evident that real poverty still exists in this country. On the other hand, it is also true that many agencies and associations, as well as the churches, are doing a great deal to alleviate the misery and apathy which such poverty breeds. Among them are Salvationists, still fulfilling the ministry of love and care which Booth and his colleagues practised.

At this point it is appropriate to pose the question as to who is responsible for ensuring that no group within this nation becomes a 'submerged tenth', such as Booth saw in the society of his day. Due to the considerable raising of expectations in more recent years, social security benefits currently available are quite often considered insufficient. The comment has already been made here about certain forms of benefit in relation to particular categories of people. But criticism of genuine efforts to ameliorate the distress of the needy is sometimes taken too far. 'Too little and too late' tends to become a kind of 'parrot-cry' for purposes of political advantage. Increasingly, thoughtful people are beginning to ask where it all ends. Who is to fund all that is being demanded, and by whom should the alleviation of human need be organised and provided? It does not follow that the government has to do it all.

It is a long and highly significant tradition that Christian charity and public-spirited philanthropy play an important role in such endeavours. Further, there is concern about the extent to which an attitude of dependence may develop among needy people if such support is provided without some thought of fostering a corresponding spirit of self-reliance. Even the idea of living within one's means is far from being generally accepted by those with lower incomes. There are tremendous pressures upon ordinary citizens to avail themselves of almost unlimited credit: 'Buy now—no payment for four months' is as immoral an invitation as it is widespread. Yet the urge to keep up with the Joneses is deep-seated. For those without the means of taking a proper holiday, possibly living in extremely drab if not unsanitary housing, the desire for a video recorder in addition to the

usual (and universal) colour television set is quite understandable. It takes your mind off your immediate surroundings and the cloud of debt which may be hanging over your
head with little prospect of being paid off.

Many such items are no longer considered optional extras.
Official statistics show that ninety-eight per cent of households in Britain have both a refrigerator and a television set.
Eighty-four per cent have a telephone and seventy-four per
cent have central heating installed. What is often lacking is
the ability—or the will—to budget for day-to-day expenses.
Many Salvation Army officers could affirm that some of
those who come to them for emergency aid have little or no
idea of how to balance the books. For some—a small
minority—there is so little money coming in that it seems
pointless trying to organise oneself. Yet only relatively few
of the deprived in our midst are dressed in real rags. Few
would forego the use of tobacco, even in times of economic
stringency. To some who have come upon hard times, it is
still unthinkable to walk any distance, or use public transport
in order to economise on travel. It is not unknown for people
claiming some form of cheap, or even free, hand-out to
arrive by taxi. This has been observed in connection with
clothing or small items of furniture available from one or
other of the Army's charity shops. It was noted particularly
when Salvation Army centres all over the country were
involved in the distribution of Common Market surplus
food stocks during the winter of 1987–88. The scale of values
of many has become strangely distorted, materially speaking. In passing, it is of interest to recall that the food in
question included butter and powdered milk valued at over
£2m, and cheese worth almost £10m also passed through
such centres during that period.

In other aspects of life, much has been achieved for the
general betterment of the majority. The National Health
Service has enhanced the quality of life and the span of life
expectancy. It has vastly diminished the incidence of several

formerly fatal diseases, especially childhood epidemics. However, other forms of illness and disease have emerged, or become more widespread. AIDS has achieved extremely high publicity because of the sheer horror of its potential without some unforeseen breakthrough in the search for an antidote. Yet this frightening new manifestation is at present still limited to a very small minority. Far more generalised are the stress-related diseases and psychosomatic illnesses. The causes are not easy to identify specifically, nor even to define. But the rat-race phenomenon of our materialistic society, without the comforting and strengthening influence of a spiritual faith, must rank high among these.

In education, too, there have been very considerable advances. Despite the criticism of low standards of achievement in a number of areas, the widespread ignorance of Victorian England, amounting often enough to sheer illiteracy, has virtually disappeared. Relatively few children have slipped through the net since the introduction of universal, compulsory free education. There remains a surprising incidence of functional illiteracy for various reasons, one of these being the very high rate of truancy. The highly publicised lack of skills in industry and commerce can more readily be traced to a failure to apply knowledge gained, or in part to irrelevant school curricula.

There is nevertheless a widespread growing concern in society, and covering the whole gamut of political persuasion, about both health and education. If either of these vital areas of national life were to become subject to market forces, with the rich gaining at the expense of the poor, it would seriously undermine the degree of progress that has been won since the inauguration of the social security system. Those most directly involved with the poorer part of the population, and concerned to help them emerge from their deprivation, are agreed on that point.

If all this progress has been achieved, and if deprivation has been at least somewhat eased, we must clearly look elsewhere to discover the sources of today's darkness. In fact, this has already been alluded to at several points in the foregoing pages. Despite all that still remains to be done to eliminate the causes of material inequality, the true darkness has its roots in the moral and spiritual dimensions of life. For Christians, and others with a firm and committed faith, that is self-evident; but perhaps far fewer than half of the population of Britain would make any such claim today. Religious education—ironically, the only compulsory subject in state schools since 1944—has been in serious decline. This trend was already evident when today's parents were at school, hence there has been widespread neglect in this vital area of life both at home and in school. Only a minority of schools hold meaningful religious assemblies or Scripture teaching. In their place we find a range of subjects variously designated as 'civics', 'the humanities' or, vaguely, 'world religions'.

In general a mood of despair, hopelessness and above all bitterness has overtaken many. This has blighted their lives and frustrated their efforts to discover and develop their true worth and identity, and to fulfil their true potential. Lack of security in employment and housing clouds the thoughts and feelings of several million of our fellow citizens. With so much reference to gaining materially, it is hardly surprising that we seem to be in danger of losing our soul—individually and nationally. Even some of the most respected enterprises in this country have climbed onto the promotional bandwagon of prize draws, with huge inducements offered. Then when material resources fail, many have little or nothing to fall back upon.

Mention has already been made of some of the evils which have enslaved people and which underlie the huge increase in violent crime. Little has changed since Booth's day as far as the prominent role of alcohol abuse is concerned in terms of criminality, as well as of accidents and personal breakdown. A vast amount of poverty can be traced to this source.

The extensive empire of commercialised and highly profitable pornography has infiltrated to the very heart of family life. The TV-video set in the living room has brought the sex-violence cinema within the range of even young children. The insidious tentacles of the drug trade have invaded even primary schools, and no group in society is exempt from the disastrous consequences of addiction. Again, the cost of indulgence has contributed very extensively to poverty. It is often the poorest people who resort to the use and abuse of drugs as a way out of the dreariness of their drab surroundings. Salvation Army personnel, with others, confirm this from their own experience as we shall see.

Not all poverty, crime or social disruption is due to evil in one form or another. Jesus' teaching that 'men love darkness rather than light, because their deeds are evil' is as true today as ever it was. However, it cannot be applied indiscriminately to all who suffer. Many are undoubtedly the victims of circumstances. These may stem from some form of mishap, error or ignorance. A great number of people reap the results of their own unwitting folly. Whatever the cause, they need help.

Redundancy can strike a family already heavily committed financially. The end result may well be re-possession of the family home due to mortgage repayment default. An unplanned pregnancy can spell disaster where both husband and wife are having to work in order to pay for all the usual expenses. Additionally, this may lead to a real conflict of conscience in having to choose between a relatively simple (but for many, morally unacceptable) abortion, or drastic domestic consequences. Again, real darkness of spirit can fall upon such a household, and the need for counsel and help can become urgent.

Despite the various safety nets of the social security system, there is a very worrying tendency in current legislation, and in governmental attitudes, towards a philosophy of 'every man for himself'—with its inevitable concomitant 'and the devil take the hindmost'.

Above all, it is impossible to escape the conclusion that a spiritual blight lies at the very roots of much of the present distress and darkness. This will become clearer as these pages present factual evidence both of decline in religious faith and practice, and of hope offered to many and accepted by some, at least.

'Light has come into the world,' wrote the author of John's Gospel about the incarnation of God in Jesus. He added, 'Whoever lives by that truth comes into the light' (Jn 3:19, 21). Christ is 'the light of men'—a light which the darkness has never been able to extinguish (Jn 1:4–5).

Therein lies the Christian's faith. Therein, too, is found the basic motivation and dynamic of today's Salvationists who, with other Christians, offer hope and practical help to those who for whatever reason have lost out in life.

Note

1. Quoted in a review commissioned by Wilfred Meynell for *Merrie England*.

3
Happy Families?

So what is the Salvation Army doing today, in darkest Britain? What forms of community-based service are operating? Is there any long-term care, and follow-up where necessary? Or is there merely emergency relief, with cups of tea? Has the pattern of William Booth's 'social wing' changed greatly over the years?

To find some answers to these questions I travelled to a number of towns and cities to see for myself. Most of my life and service as a Salvation Army officer has been spent abroad. Thus in retirement I was interested to learn more about what Booth's present-day successors are doing in this country. The broad outlines were familiar to me, but I did not know all the details of the day-to-day front-line drama being enacted in and through the movement's multiple programmes. I learned through asking questions, through personal observation and to a lesser degree through correspondence. I discovered more in conversation with those directly involved in the oversight of the Army's work in the United Kingdom.

I hope that my observations and reflections will be both challenging and encouraging. Challenging because of what they reveal about our society today; encouraging because of what my fellow Salvationists, together with many committed Christians and other concerned people, are doing about it.

First, a few details about the Army's organisational structures may be helpful. Its socalled 'social' and 'field' operations have evolved along separate but parallel lines, for quite practical reasons. They are nevertheless still under one overall leadership, and increasingly close working relationships are being forged. The work of the Salvation Army Social Services includes virtually all residential programmes, operating in more than 130 centres through-out the country —and including a small work in the Republic of Ireland. Here and there some nonresidential service is provided, notably the Investigations (Missing Persons) Department, and the nationwide prison chaplaincy services.

The 'field' work means, in Salvationist language, the corps (churches) with their congregations, totalling some 53,500 soldiers (full members), and their varied activities. There are around 850 such congregations in Britain. Most of them are small—meaning with fewer than 100 soldiers, but they are none the less dedicated in their work and witness.

This branch of Army work also includes the twenty-nine goodwill centres—successors to the former slum posts, still working in urban areas of deprivation. Just a handful of the field centres have some kind of short-term emergency residential accommodation—usually seasonal, in winter. Most do not and are quite simply community-centred.

Two independent housing associations are registered in the Army's name, one covering England and Wales and the other based in Scotland. Both use the Army's Social Services as agents for a variety of residential homes and hostels, but also operate their own schemes, such as sheltered housing. Both are mainly funded, like other housing associations these days, by the government's Housing Corporation. The programme envisaged for any individual centre to be capital-financed through the housing association is predetermined in close and amicable consultation.

The Social Services have benefited very considerably from

such financial input, but they have retained full freedom to operate in accordance with the Army's principles and its spiritual priorities. Moreover, these are known and respected by the various public authorities concerned. The majority of the work of the Army's Social Services is still funded from within the movement.

The establishment of a training centre at Chislehurst, Kent, in 1982 and a smaller unit in Glasgow has done much to enhance the professional quality of the social work. A number of officers and others comprising the staff of the various centres had already gained degrees or diplomas in social work. Now wide-ranging residential courses provide in-service training for a large percentage of the more than 2,000 employees within this branch of Army work. All this, of course, goes hand in hand with what is sometimes referred to as sanctified common sense and sheer compassion.

The family is the basic unit in the structure of society, so all Christians must be deeply concerned about the quality of family life within the nation. Thus they will do everything possible to offer support and practical help for families in any kind of need. This also includes 'repair' operations where families break up. Salvationists have long been in the forefront of such action as a result of William Booth's insistence that his soldiers were 'saved to serve'.

The majority of the Army's Social Services centres are concerned in one way or another with families, whether intact or fragmented. The majority of homeless people who arrive at hostels come from broken homes. Residential centres for the elderly—known as eventide homes—are more necessary than ever at a time when the wider family group has lost much of its former cohesion. The reasons are often simple enough. Family housing is seldom adequate in terms of modern expectations to take in grandma and grandpa or elderly maiden aunts, as often happened in the past. Thus for those who reach the age or stage of no longer being able to manage by themselves, such homes are a real haven in the later years of life. They also ease the moral and practical concerns of the children of residents, who may be struggling to maintain their own families intact.

The considerable increase in the fostering of children has seen a corresponding decline in children's homes. There are, of course, still several voluntary agencies specialising in the care of children, some of them with a definite Christian background. For some concerned people, it is an open question whether the trend towards fostering will ultimately prove genuinely satisfactory for children separated from their families. In any event, the Army still maintains four children's centres, three of which are registered as community homes for children. Inevitably, all of them are constantly involved with families in crisis.

Centres for adolescents are small-scale residential homes to which teenagers may be referred or committed by local authority social workers, probation officers or magistrates in the juvenile courts. These are youngsters who, in most cases, never had a chance. They can no longer be left in their family homes, for whatever reason. Nevertheless, every attempt is made to involve the parents right from the initial referral. Both the Army's adolescent units in Britain at present are in Scotland, with a third in Dublin (see p 99).

In half a dozen cities around the country, the Salvation Army has centres specifically designed for families in crisis circumstances. There are also several places catering for women, often with children, who are at risk. The danger is usually related to marital discord, leading all too often to violence by the man. (Sometimes the tables are turned, we learn, and the man becomes a target for flying objects hurled by his enraged spouse!)

The outreach of the Salvation Army's field services in Britain also touches very widely upon family life. As noted earlier, these are basically non-residential. The more conventional of them may not usually be associated in the public mind with 'bringing light into darkened corners of society'. Yet even the clubs for over-sixties (variously called 'silver threads', 'golden age' or similar names), and the various kinds of luncheon or day-care clubs meet a deeply felt need, especially among older people. Loneliness and social isolation can be very dark experiences, especially in areas of social deprivation, and in the increasingly impersonal and anonymous nature of urban life. Hence such groups undoubtedly help very considerably to brighten many an otherwise sombre life-pattern. While offering a family atmosphere to those separated in one way or another from their own families, these activities have a definite spiritual content. Quite a number of members have become real Christians as a result of attendance, with all the transforming effects of the new life in Christ as members of the family of God.

Groups catering for parents (usually mothers) and toddlers are being established on an expanding scale. Some of the young women who attend are single mums who have either suffered a marriage breakdown or have never married. Most of them experience real stress in one form or another, though some come simply for companionship. Many are trying to maintain themselves economically while caring for one or more children. Others are struggling to come to terms with undesired motherhood, and with little or no domestic support. A number have themselves been abused as children or have lacked the love and stimulation so essential to normal development. A surprising number simply have no idea even how to play with their children. At present some 200 corps operate such a programme, usually on a weekly basis. More than 2,000 women share in these occasions nationally each week.

Additionally, organised groups exist in several Army corps aimed at providing respite care of physically or mentally handicapped people. A few corps cater for victims of strokes or heart attacks, with all the physical and emotional limitations they create. Yet others offer facilities for the young unemployed, aimed in the first place at keeping them off the streets, but ultimately at some measure of ongoing support. Here and there attempts are being made to help jobless and aimless alcoholics on a day-time, first-aid basis. In some instances this may eventually lead to more specialised, probably residential, care in one of the Army's ten centres across the country, which are equipped to offer such treatment.

It will be seen that each of the foregoing categories of programme, attempting to respond meaningfully to a variety of needs, impinges upon family life. In the following chapters we shall look at individual examples of such activities.

The needs of handicapped people have been exposed in recent years. The importance of easy access to all sorts of public buildings for such people has been highlighted. It was therefore quite natural that the Salvation Army should establish its own Association for the Handicapped in 1968. Membership is open to all handicapped children and adults, and their carers, whether or not they have any other links with the Army. At present there are around 750 members. The Association is affiliated to the Central Council for the Disabled.

Various activities are organised, designed to create interest, stimulation and therapy. These include holidays (with volunteer care staff), camps, festivals and sports meetings. Equally important, the national secretary maintains personal links with members by sending each one a birthday and Christmas card annually. A monthly newsletter is also issued which contains various items of news and comment combined with useful information for the disabled, culled from documentation issued by national organisations specialising in such matters. These include MENCAP and RADAR (Royal Association for Disability and Rehabilitation).

More than a hundred copies of a sixty-minute taped version of the Army's newsletter are sent each month to blind and partially sighted members. A Braille version of the Army's songbook (nearly a thousand songs!) was prepared by a prisoner serving a life sentence, as part of his work therapy in prison. His story can be found in Chapter 10. The Braille songbook was subsequently produced by the Royal National Institute for the Blind, and is available free to any visually handicapped member.

In many instances members of this association are linked up with another Salvation Army service, the League of Mercy. This long-established programme originally consisted mainly of hospital visitation by local Salvationists. It has now been broadened to cover home visits to sick, housebound or otherwise deprived people. Homes for the elderly, nursing homes, sheltered housing complexes and similar centres regularly receive Salvationists who come to offer friendship and practical help of various kinds, for instance letter-writing or shopping. Local prisons may be visited, though we have already noted that there is a separate network of chaplaincy services covering a hundred of the country's main prisons.

The largest and perhaps best-known corps section of the Army, both in Britain and in the ninety other countries where the movement is at work, is the Home League. The fourfold aim of this 350,000-strong women's movement, with around 70,000 members in Britain, embraces education and service in addition to fellowship and worship. The teaching element, designed to enhance the quality of homes, and hence of families, has been a tremendous success since its inception in 1907. One writer has described it as 'one of the most powerful influences for good the Army has produced'.

Its annual Helping Hand projects have created extensive opportunities for service to others, and raised large sums of money for Army work at home and abroad. Best of all, thousands of women have found Christ as Saviour, and their homes have then been transformed. After all, mother is still at the heart of family life!

The centrality of family life in society is amply reflected in the loving care shown by thousands of Salvationists from all walks of life, in a variety of programmes.

Before looking further at this range of caring services, it is important to remind ourselves of the general background to family life in our country today. To begin with, there is no longer one accepted definition of the word 'family'. Instead, there is talk of a variety of types of family. What was once taken for granted as a family: father, mother and one or more children, is now spoken of as the 'nuclear' family. Alongside this definition, the concept of the 'extended' family is still valid, even though links are looser than they used to be. This embraces a wider unit comprising three generations of close relatives, including one or more nuclear families. The majority of families in Britain still fall within one or other of these categories.

However, a substantial minority of family groups now have to be defined in other terms. Single-parent families have become so numerous as to be considered almost normal. In 1986, fourteen per cent of dependent children in the United Kingdom lived in such family groups—twice the 1972 figure. This modern social trend naturally arouses widespread alarm. What will it mean for the future, thinking particularly of the children who are brought up in such potential deprivation? Much sympathy and many forms of practical help and counsel are, very rightly, available to single parents nowadays. Even central government legislation has had to be amended to take in the needs of such incomplete families.

Nevertheless, the very term 'one-parent family' is a contradiction in terms. If the old saying is true, that 'it takes two to make a quarrel', it is much more fundamentally and demonstrably true that it requires two individuals, male and female, to create a new human life. This is the basic and natural pattern of human life.

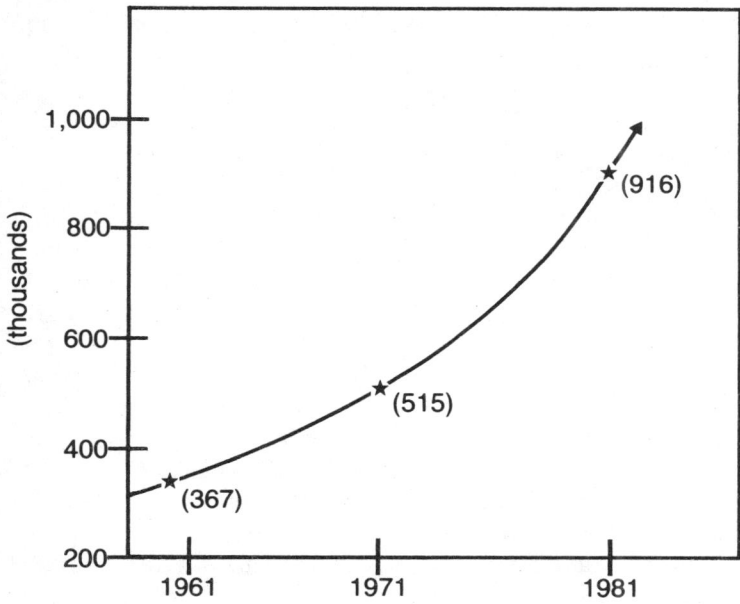

Single parent families with dependent children

Problems are never lacking even in the best managed of normal families, of course. However, the difficulties increase very sharply when either the natural (biological) mother or father is missing. This may occur when either partner (usually the man) is absent for long periods: for instance, in connection with employment. It also happens when the father abdicates his responsibilities, which should be equal and complementary to those of the mother. Again the quite bizarre vogue introduced by some extreme feminists, to consider men as irrelevant once they have sired a child, is matched only by the much older problem of male chauvinism. Both are equally abhorrent, and injurious to children.

It is worth noting that the term 'one-parent family' includes those where one spouse has died, just as much as those where the parental relationship has suffered rupture, whether temporary or permanent. In the former case, the fact that the father or mother is no longer alive may actually help the child. In contrast, there is great confusion in the mind of a child when the missing parent is known to be around, and possibly in fairly regular contact.

There is further complication when remarriage takes place, thus introducing the child into the step-family. Well handled, the forming of a two-parent family (a heterosexual couple) in this way can be very therapeutic. Happily, this is often the case. In many cases, however, children suffer varying degrees of trauma in attempting to adjust to a new father or mother. A notable fact in this connection is the widespread sexual or other abuse practised by some step parents, mostly the man (see Chapter 4).

Further definitions of family include 'teenage families', meaning that the parents are still of that age. Biologically quite capable of procreation, they are usually unprepared emotionally and economically to create and nurture a family. There are also 'homosexual families', where both adult members of the household are of the same sex, usually women. Clearly, only one of these is the true mother of any child, who has nevertheless chosen to live in this unnatural and unhealthy manner, thereby subjecting the child(ren) to the same abnormal social influences.

Similarly, there are some 'communal families', where 'all things are held in common'—including, sometimes, the sexual partners. Such evidence as exists suggests that for children born into these surroundings there is ultimately a good deal of confusion and emotional deprivation. They belong to no one parent in particular and may grow up quite seriously maladjusted. It is noteworthy that the Israeli pioneers of *kibbutz* life discovered this problem after some years, even in the otherwise strictly ordered life of those communities.

It is evident that the disruption to national life through the erosion of clear psychological, emotional and moral guidelines and norms will be very considerable. Here, too, the availability of guidance and counsel for those willing to receive it is a major contribution to the stability of the nation.

How is it that the pattern of family life which, for all its individual instances of breakdown, has been the strength of our society for so long is now seriously threatened? Of course, divorce is not a new factor in human relationships. It was spoken of in ancient times, and there are several biblical references to it. Some Christians today are still completely opposed to divorce for any reason other than adultery. They interpret the teaching of Jesus very literally, and one can respect their sincerity and integrity. Better such an attitude than the 'anything goes' approach so often encountered.

For centuries the church was the sole arbiter of the dissolution of marriages. During the nineteenth century, however, secular legislation was adopted in Britain, setting out the terms and conditions for terminating the marriage relationship. Most Christians, together with many others, still felt that divorce was an indication of failure, and that some stigma was attached to the divorced state. This attitude still persists today in certain quarters, but the scale on which divorce is now conducted is a distinctly modern phenomenon. Clearly the liberalisation of this country's divorce laws has been a major factor.

In 1973 a new Matrimonial Causes Act became law, incorporating radical reforms enacted in 1965 and 1969. The situation changed almost overnight. The only reason for ending a marriage now was 'the irretrievable breakdown' of the relationship. Divorce could be granted by mutual consent, after two years of living apart. Failing such agreement, the termination might be granted after five years of separation. So-called 'quickie' divorces were possible even more rapidly under a 'special procedure'. The majority of petitioners now use this approach. Thus the flood-gates have been opened wide. The procedures were further liberalised when, in 1984, the Matrimonial and Family Proceedings Act was approved by parliament. Now a partner could sue for divorce so long as the marriage had lasted at least a year. Britain now has the highest divorce rate in the European Community, ahead of Denmark and the Netherlands. Further, the rate of increase of divorce in the UK is the highest in Europe.

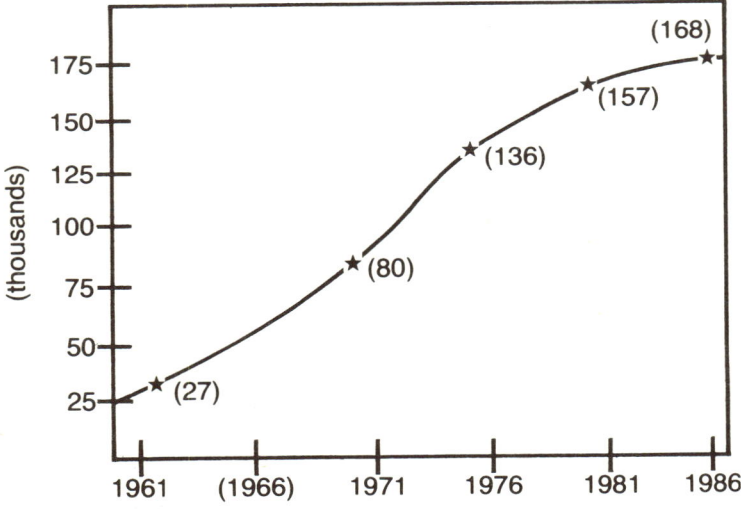

Divorces (decrees made absolute) — UK

In fact, there no longer remains any *de facto* moral basis to divorce proceedings. In most instances the conduct of the partners is virtually ignored. One legal expert has written: 'People consider it important that the legal system should administer justice rather than simple rules of division.'[1] A number of reformers continue to press the point that the present approach in law runs counter to people's moral instincts. The notion of a 'no-fault' break-up of marriage is, in the great majority of cases, quite false to the facts, given the nature of the marriage vows. The issue is of course highly complex and very sensitive. It touches upon some of the most intimate areas of human relationships. Yet it is abundantly clear that things have gone badly awry in recent years. It is equally evident that something will have to change if we are to avoid further serious collapse of family life, thus gravely affecting society as a whole.

On the positive side, many couples who had endured a 'living hell', because divorce was not possible for them, were now 'liberated'. The opportunity of starting a new life was suddenly theirs. In the name of all that is humane and compassionate, that could only be a good thing. Unhappily, official published figures show very clearly that many such second marriages have again failed—quite rapidly, in some instances.

A whole series of consequences now unfolded: some foreseen, others not. Statistically, the number of divorces increased dramatically from 58,000 in 1970 to 160,000 in 1985. During the same period the number of marriages registered declined from just over 415,000 in 1970 to a little more than 346,000 in 1985. Almost certainly those figures do not mean that fewer couples 'wedded', but rather that cohabitation had become much more widespread. The desperate longing for emotional security, together with the deeply felt urge for sexual activity, lead so many into the folly of cohabitation without commitment. It is perhaps easier to commit oneself to a principle of philosophy than to another human being, 'for better or worse'!

Official published figures show that the number of women aged eighteen to twenty-four cohabitating has increased from four-and-a-half per cent in 1979 to eleven-and-a-half per cent in 1987. The rise is somewhat less pronounced in the twenty-five to forty-nine-year-old group: from just over two per cent in 1979 to four-and-a-half per cent in 1987. It has to be said that some of these partnerships are quite stable, and appear to last at least as well as many marriages. However, the experience of Salvation Army staff working in this field suggests a very considerable rise in the number of extremely fragile relationships in this category.

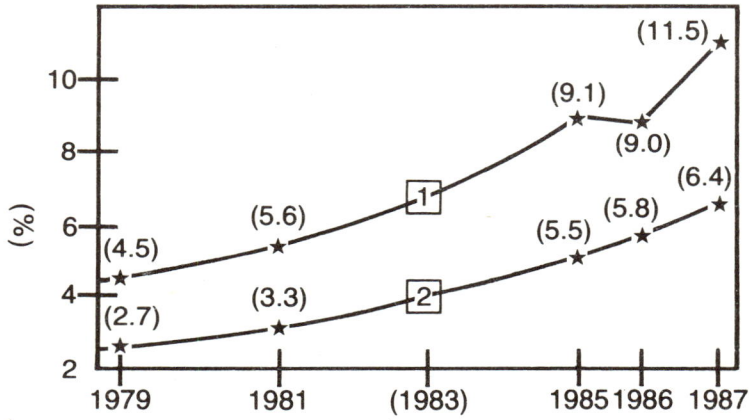

Women co-habiting
1   as a percentage of all women aged 18–49 years;
2   as a percentage of women aged 18–24 years.

Add to all this the consequences of separation and divorce for the children of a union, and it is hardly surprising that such rapid erosion of family structures has taken place in just a few years. More than 150,000 children are now affected every year by the divorce of their parents. It is estimated that one child in every four born today is likely to see his parents separate before he reaches the age of eighteen.

It has already been suggested that children react more negatively to the separation of their parents than to the death of one or the other. The bitterness which precedes many divorces, and the tension experienced during the proceedings, may scar a child emotionally for a very long time.

Critical comment by the parent having custody of the child about the other parent only adds to the overwhelming confusion and stress.

Children generally react badly when they see strife between their parents. When separation occurs they very often become deeply resentful and angry. For one thing, they may quickly lose all contact with the family of the non-custodial parent, thus experiencing a kind of 'kinship amputation'. Some fantasise about their parents coming together again, while others tend to withdraw into themselves at a stage in their growth when social contacts are vital to the development of their life skills. It is interesting to note that at the time of writing, a serious proposal has been made to amend the law so that grandparents would have a greater say in the continuing practical arrangements for the children of divorcing parents. Most of all, such children fear the possibility of losing the remaining parent too. This fear may find expression in a variety of behavioural aberration—when others will say, 'It's not like her,' or 'He's not himself these days.' Of course they're not! How can they be? In a very real sense the bottom has fallen out of their world at a time when they are emotionally both immature and highly vulnerable.

Among the thousands of youngsters whom Salvationists, and others concerned with the homeless, encounter are a high proportion who simply left home because of marital feuding, or complete breakdown of their parents' relationships. Yet others have been turned out of house and home, having been found 'unacceptable' by a step-parent. The turmoil which this has created in them is now reflected in their behaviour as they come together with others in the same situation. Aggressiveness, inverted hatred and anger, often directed inwardly, unquestionably account for a great deal of the behavioural pattern among the young, which society then criticises.

Among the young women—some still in their middle

teens—who pass through Salvation Army (and other) centres, as being 'at risk' (we used to say, much more realistically, 'in moral danger'), are many whose ability to relate to others has been seriously undermined by the trauma of parental conflict in their own homes. We will look at this more fully when discussing the work in such homes.

The root of so much social and emotional upheaval is that children feel unwanted, rejected, and sacrificed on the altar of their parents' selfish preoccupation with their own feelings. The whole process looks more and more like a continuing blight in society. Above all, children need to feel loved, wanted, cared for—even if their attitudes sometimes appear to belie that fact. Yet so often it is precisely those feelings which are thwarted by the divorce proceedings of the growing army of adults who seek a way out of a relationship for which they lack a deeper commitment. The truth remains, divorce is not an easy option.

It is not unusual in schools—even Sunday schools—to hear children talking together in an apparently nonchalant way about past and present parents. In some cases a parent has passed from one child in such a group to another. 'When your dad used to live with us' is one variant of such exchanges, as children struggle inwardly to come to terms with what has happened. Yet in their moments of emotional vulnerability and tenderness (especially at bed-time!), the nonchalance evaporates. The simple and unchangeable fact is that children need *both* parents for the balanced development of their personality, and their ability to find a personal identity. This naturally includes their sexual identity, and here again the role model of father or mother, for boy or girl, is crucially important.

The range of problems associated with children will be discussed in Chapter 4. They are extremely grave in terms of the nature of society in the future, and the harm being done cannot be quickly or easily undone. But for the present we will confine this enquiry to the broader canvas of family life.

In common with Christians everywhere, the Salvation Army deplores current trends. At the same time it has to be said that these trends have not left the Army itself untouched. A sad number of Salvationists have themselves been involved in divorce proceedings, as has happened in virtually all churches today. However, as a movement the Army has felt it necessary to respond to invitations to comment on moral, social and spiritual issues.

In a letter to the Law Commission, in October 1988, the Army's leadership made certain recommendations through the then Legal Secretary, Major Shaw Clifton. These concerned future changes in the divorce laws, in response to a working document sent out to a variety of public bodies. The Commission's discussion paper, *Facing the Future*, contained a number of suggestions relating to the reduction of stress in divorce proceedings, commensurate with the maximum effort possible to avoid final rupture of a marriage. Basing its response upon 'the Army's extensive experience of involvement with families under stress, and with spouses whose marriages either are breaking down or have broken down', the document's general contents were welcomed.

One of the points referred to is the unfairness which may affect an 'innocent' spouse when, 'in order to avoid undue prolongation of the proceedings, that partner must put up with the accusations of "unreasonable behaviour"—those accusations being known to be falsely based'. 'Unreasonable behaviour' is one of the three grounds in present legislation which, leading to the 'irretrievable breakdown' of a marriage, may be cited by the petitioner.

As far back as 1987, the *New Law Journal* commented on the statistics published by the Office of Population Censuses and Surveys, in respect of divorces. It noted that 'the percentage of divorces on the grounds of behaviour has increased considerably. .... The behaviour ground remains the most unsatisfactory from both a substantive and procedural point of view, but also the most popular because it allows an immediate petition.'

It is precisely this point of 'undue haste' which is at the heart of the Army's attitude towards eventual amendments to the present law. 'Whilst the Army would not wish to advocate changes ... which would render divorce more difficult to obtain than at present, it is felt that present procedures permit the overall process to be completed too swiftly.' There is not enough time for the parties to adjust emotionally or psychologically to their new circumstances. Also, the Army would welcome reforms in the law designed to minimise the bitterness which characterises so many divorces at present.

From the various options set out in the Law Commission's document, the Army opted for a nine-month waiting period following the submission of a divorce petition, before commencement of the proceedings. This represents a shorter time-scale than many reformers would wish for, but longer than others proposed. It is a considered compromise, taking all factors into account.

Still related to the reduction of hurried proceedings, and the consequent minimalisation of efforts at reconciliation, the Salvation Army wishes to see the government allocate major funding to provide realistic counselling resources. It is felt that present procedures do not specifically cater for such guidance and conciliation help. While recognising that counselling is normally effective only when voluntarily accepted, the Army's leaders feel that the offer of such facilities of the highest professional quality should have maximum priority in future proceedings. Where reconciliation is ultimately not possible, conciliation can help avoid a great deal of conflict and tension, bitterness and recrimination.

It is of more than passing interest here to note that William

Booth's son, Bramwell, who had succeeded him as the Army's General, set up a Reconciliation Department as early as 1926.

> I am anxious to establish [such a] department in addition to the Anti-Suicide Bureau [established in 1907]. There is a special need for reconciliation, such as between a man and wife who have been separated. Someone is needed who will step in wisely and kindly, bringing about a reconciliation instead of leaving the parties concerned to the miserable procedure of divorce.

With this announcement by its leader, the Salvation Army once again initiated procedures which would later be incorporated into the social support facilities in the country.

Nearly 10,000 applications were dealt with in the first full year of the new department's operation. No detailed analysis of this total is available, but about a quarter of the first 300 cases were successful in effecting genuine reconciliation. Another seventy-five per cent were 'helped and advised'.

Commenting at the conclusion of that year, the head of the department stated:

> We cannot always effect a reconciliation ... We have been asked [to do so in circumstances] which would only mean worse trouble later. Kindly, but firmly, we were able to show that separation or divorce was really best in the interests of the innocent sufferer, or the welfare of the children.

In 1979, General Arnold Brown issued a statement on behalf of the Army, *Family Policy in the United Kingdom*. In it he said:

> Legislation cannot abolish selfishness, intolerance or waywardness, which in our view contribute more to the breakdown of marriages than poverty or poor housing. The Salvation Army's experience suggests that a great many marriages that now break down could be saved, and the parties find fulfilment for

themselves and security for their children, given a willingness to persevere and a measure of social support at times of
crisis.

Today a growing number of the Army's officers undergo
training in marriage guidance counselling as part of their
pastoral ministry.

These details are set down simply to record that the
Salvation Army does more than offer practical help of
many kinds to people in need. A considerable amount
of high-level lobbying of government departments and
members of parliament is undertaken. Representations are
made on subjects with which the Army has close contact
through its very considerable network of social centres
and community-based programmes. Such pressure is based
upon Christian ethical and spiritual standards, in the belief
that governments have a responsibility to set standards, at
least as much as to legislate according to popular sentiment
and opinion. In other words there should be a 'theocratic'
as well as a democratic element in the ordering of these
very basic issues which so profoundly affect the nation's
highest welfare.

Other questions relating to family life, on which Salvation
Army leadership has taken a clear and positive stand, include abortion and the prescription of contraceptives for
girls under the age of sixteen without the knowledge of
their parents. On this latter issue, the Army very actively
supported Mrs Victoria Gillick in her courageous campaign against legislative amendments proposed by the then
Department of Health and Social Security. Only at the very
last stage was an earlier verdict in her favour overturned by
the Law Lords—on appeal to the House of Lords. The Court
of Appeal had unanimously ruled that parents have the full
right to know if and when contraceptives are to be made
available to their under-age daughters.

Even this setback does not alter the Army's stance on the

vital nature of protection for those most vulnerable in society. It seems a very curious anomaly, to say the least, that parents should be excluded from discussion on so important a matter affecting their impressionable and immature children, when the general tenor of much government comment on family matters is to emphasise parental responsibility. Parental consent is still required even for a tonsils operation, but not for prescription of the contraceptive pill with its inherent dangers.

Further, to condone the use of contraceptives in this way for girls with whom it is illegal to have sexual intercourse, appears to be an encouragement to breach the law. It was the Salvation Army which, in 1885, was directly responsible for the passing of an act of parliament raising the age of consent for girls from thirteen to sixteen years. An intensive nationwide campaign was conducted, with particular support from W T Stead, editor of the *Pall Mall Gazette*. The so-called Maiden Tribute affair owed its impetus to Bramwell Booth and his wife, Florence. Bramwell, together with Stead, personally investigated the sordid traffic in young girls who were procured for immoral purposes. (The law of that time held that any girl of thirteen years or over was a 'consenting adult in sexual intercourse'.) Their findings were subsequently highlighted and aroused enormous public outrage, as well as opposition from those (some in very high places!) with a vested interest in that vile trade. Stead was actually sentenced to three months' imprisonment, on a technicality, but the outcome was the amendment to British law on the subject.

In the light of the Gillick campaign, one is entitled to ask whether we as a nation have not lowered our standards in such matters in the course of the past 100 years. Research suggests that at least fifty per cent of sixteen-year-old girls today are already sexually active, while fewer than ten per cent of women are virgins on their (first) wedding day. In this connection doctors are pointing out that the risk of cervical cancer in later life is greatly increased the earlier girls begin to have sexual relations.

The age of consent remains sixteen years, and this is also the legal minimum age for marriage in this country. It is therefore worth noting here, in conclusion, that the Salvation Army has suggested to the Law Commission that it might be timely to commence public discussion on the possibility of raising the age at which people can marry. It is universally recognised that marriages entered into at a relatively early age face a much higher statistical probability of breakdown than those taking place at a somewhat later age. In any event, the overall priority remains the support and protection of the family, to ensure its integrity and enhance the quality of family life.

On the question of abortion, the Army's position emphasises the sanctity of all human life as a gift from God. The principle of abortion on demand is completely rejected. However, in certain clearly defined circumstances, termination of a pregnancy may be justified.

These include a pregnancy which is judged by competent medical and allied staff to pose a serious threat to the life of the mother, or could result in irreversible physical injury to the mother. In cases of proven rape or legally defined incest, the fact that rape and incest violate the whole person is deemed sufficient justification for termination. Also, where it is clear that a foetal abnormality exists which is likely to lead to no more than very brief survival after birth, or where a complete lack of intelligence and awareness (cognitive function) is shown to be the outcome of allowing the pregnancy to go to term, abortion would be morally justifiable.

However, the Army views the question much more broadly than the relatively simple surgical intervention to terminate a pregnancy. Salvationists know only too well that there are deep and often unforeseen emotional consequences. Hence when an abortion has taken place, The Salvation

Army will respond with loving and compassionate care. The Army is aware that abortion is regarded by some as just another means of contraception, but denies the validity of such a viewpoint. The Army's principles enshrine the ideals of chastity before marriage and fidelity within the marriage relationship. Such a clearcut declaration is all the more necessary and relevant in today's morally permissive atmosphere in which virtually anything is found acceptable to so many.

It is perhaps appropriate to record here that in 1987, twenty-one per cent of all live births were outside marriage. The figure for 1980 was twelve per cent. Some of what were formerly referred to as 'illegitimate births' (many sources still use the phrase) are the issue of quite stable relationships, when the names of both parents appear on the birth certificate. Since the hasty enactment of the 1987 Family Law Reform Act, no reference is made on those certificates to the marital status of the parents, thus effectively removing the legal distinction between legitimate and illegitimate children.

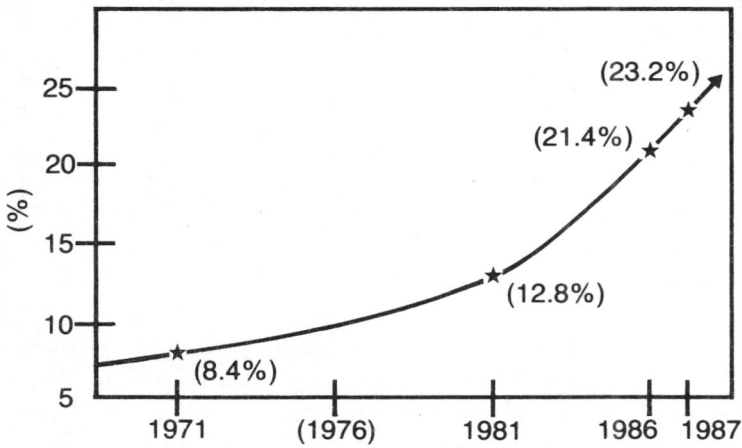

Births outside marriage (as a percentage of all live births)

Long and varied experience in many countries, commencing in Britain, involving women who do not want to bring yet another child into the world, has not led Salvationists to feel that abortion is actually the easiest solution. It is their experience that where unwanted pregnancies occur, in most instances it is best to counsel acceptance of the situation by all involved. This includes carrying the foetus to term, and for all possible supportive help to be given. When teenage girls, sometimes as young as twelve and thirteen years, find themselves pregnant and therefore in real difficulty, they find that supportive care in the Army's centres for girls and young women. The combination of professional insight into the true dilemma of such girls and a deeply spiritual desire to help them come to terms with it, form the basis of the help offered.

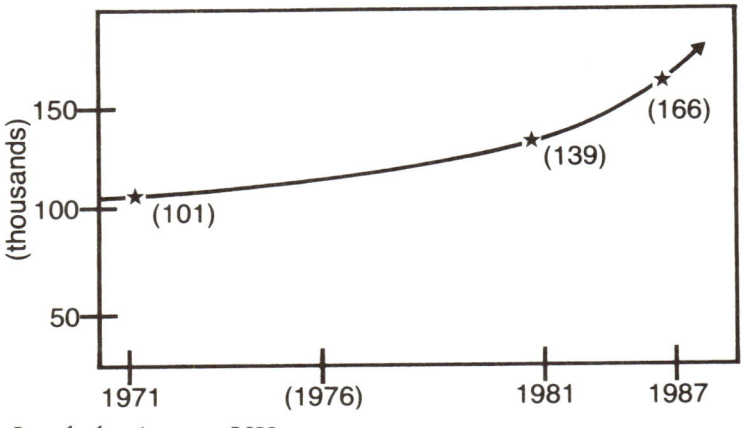

Legal abortions — UK

In all aspects of life, the aim of society must be to provide all that is needed to enable all its members to achieve their fullest potential. Where such development does not take place, for whatever reason, society itself is weakened. Where such weakness occurs on a scale which creates the threat of disintegration from within, it is time to speak out—and to act.

There is a good deal of evidence to suggest that we have reached such a point in Britain. When family life and all the closer and more intimate human relationships are threatened, as they appear to be today, it can well be said that we live in 'darkened' times. But there is light. Hope can be discerned wherever there are people whose contribution to the community helps to strengthen the 'wholeness' and 'togetherness' in which each individual can reach towards that fullest potential. And the strongest and most effective force to help achieve that goal remains—love.

Note

1. Professor Stephen Cretney, in evidence to the Special Standing Committee on the Matrimonial and Family Proceedings Bill (1984), quoted by George Brown in *Families Matter* (Marshall Pickering: Basingstoke, 1987), p 145.

4
Suffer the Children

Today's Western society has given a very prominent position to the young in its midst. 'Kids rule, OK?' may be meant half humorously, but the moral viewpoint it reflects is unique in history. The demands and rights of children and adolescents are taken seriously by adults in general. Fashions in clothing, tastes in music and art, together with the availability of enough money to indulge their habits and fulfil their wishes, are all significant matters today.

Young people are being encouraged to save money. At the same time they are being tempted by banks and similar institutions with a range of credit facilities. They are introduced into the world of 'little plastic cards' before they start regularly earning. Parents often feel under considerable pressure to spend increasing sums on Christmas, birthday and other gifts for their children. To deal with this, they too engage in long-term credit. It has become a way of life. The most important thing is to give the children what they want. And why not?

Yet we have already noted that on quite another plane society has made possible a large-scale breakdown in the pattern of emotional security which family life is supposed to provide. Some of the basic facts referred to in Chapter 3 show conclusively that very many children and adolescents are currently being denied the normal birthright of every such young person: love, care, and security. Indeed, 'betrayal' is not too strong a word for this failure to ensure the basics of life for those whom we bring into the world. Why?

Some years ago, in the course of an international conference dealing with what was then referred to as the population explosion, warnings were given about the long-term consequences of present demographic trends. One comment which attracted a good deal of media attention at the time was made by a delegate from the People's Republic of China. 'Our children are our greatest riches' was the gist of his remark.

Of all nations, China has had urgent cause to consider its rapidly growing population, and the results of a continuing increase. Since the conference in question, the government of that vast nation has introduced, and tried legally to enforce, a policy of severe restriction on families. Only one child per family was to be allowed—by law. Where a second pregnancy occurred pressure was brought to bear upon the mother. Abortion was advocated and dire consequences threatened by party officials if the parents did not respond.

Not surprisingly, the policy has proved unenforceable, at least in many parts of this the world's most populous state. However, one can understand the point of view of the nation's leaders, once they realised the effects of an uncontrolled, rapidly rising birth rate. To allow a huge expansion of the problem was simply unthinkable.

Even more desperate is the plight of many developing countries, where drought and famine, ignorance of basic hygiene, civil war, or some kind of natural or man-made disaster mean that millions of children die unnecessarily every year. In these lands, the problem of over-population is well taken care of by what is sometimes called 'natural selection'. Yet here we are in relatively prosperous Britain—with all our material resources and highly developed technology allied with advanced knowledge—failing to provide for the deepest needs of our young. None of us would deny the truth expressed by the Chinese that children *are* the greatest riches of any society. They guarantee the survival of a nation and its culture. They are the way forward for the human race. The quality of life in the future is almost entirely dependent upon the way today's young people are brought up and influenced. But what are we offering them? Large hunks of indigestible materialism, but only a few crumbs of moral and spiritual comfort, it seems.

Most parents and other adults are doing their best to teach and train their children. They try to keep a balance between the massive emphasis on material acquisition and the need for emotional and psychological stability. They try to apply enough discipline to ensure that their children will be able to relate well to others. That is not easy in today's world where young people insist upon their rights.

Education has seen considerable changes over the past few decades. Some have been for the better, while others have been counter-productive. Compulsory universal education in Britain has not realised the utopian ideals of the initiators of the 1944 Education Act. The expression 'preparation for life' begs the question as to what sort of life we have in mind.

By and large, schools have not provided the support and reinforcement of home life which is an important part of their role. Great efforts are currently being made to redress this imbalance, and there is a growing awareness of the need for home and school, parent and teacher, to work more closely together. The imparting of knowledge, or training in methods of study, are not sufficient in isolation. Without a framework of order and discipline, and an awareness of inter-personal relationships, such teaching has relatively little value. It will not help to develop good citizens. It cannot really improve the quality of life within our society.

Many people throughout the world today regard authority as something to be rejected, even aggressively opposed. Future historians may come to see this attitude as an integral part of the huge social revolution of our age. One possible cause of such an attitude may well be found in some of the parents of today. There was a considerable reaction against officialdom and discipline, militarism and violence, following the ending of hostilities in 1945. Democracy was the key to the future, and for some that meant they could do as they wished. There are undoubtedly more families than we imagine in which children are positively encouraged 'not to let them push you around'.

While most schools are well ordered, with good teacher-pupil relationships, that is by no means true everywhere. The teaching profession is alarmed at the increase in pupil violence, either as wanton vandalism or in assaults on fellow pupils or members of staff. One researcher recently published the findings of his enquiries into this area of the educational system. 'Teachers have to regain their authority. There has been a general attitude that all forms of authority are wrong, and that has done a lot of harm to relationships between adults and children.'[1] He might have added that the whole of society has been harmed by such false notions.

The report goes on: 'Teachers need to be authoritative rather than authoritarian'—a subtle but significant distinction which most people see as axiomatic. The background to this research was bullying in schools. This has resulted in at least one death in a British school, and in widespread fear among many thousands of children. One major conclusion is summed up thus: 'The biggest single factor in determining whether a child became a bully (violent and aggressive) was the attitude of parents. Children whose parents were too busy to care, and who were given too much freedom, were likely to become bullies.'

The link between the influence of home and family on the

one hand, and school and education on the other, is reflected in very many communities. There is more than a suspicion that some parents are genuinely afraid of their own children's potential for violence.

These comments apply to a minority, of course. Yet it is a sizeable and worrying minority. At a time when the incidence of crime in general is decreasing, criminal violence is on the increase. In particular, sexual and other violent assaults are growing in number—and in viciousness. Literally millions of women live in fear of being raped. They carry personal security alarms in their handbags, or attend self-defence classes. Even women in their eighties have been subjected to unspeakable atrocities, and quite often it is teenagers who commit such crimes. In one recent instance, three pre-teenage boys were involved in such an attack.

A young blind man is viciously attacked by a gang of young men in a London suburban train in broad daylight. One teenage pupil murders another of different racial origin in a school playground. Damage totalling millions of pounds is caused by juvenile arsonists. These are not isolated events; they occur with alarming regularity, and society seems unable to curb the mindless and brutal behaviour of this turbulent criminal minority. By the time this book is published there will be more such up-to-date incidents—a grotesque euphemism for appalling tragedies. Tragedies on both sides. Not only are innocent people more and more likely to become victims of aggression at the hands of adolescents and even children, those youngsters also represent a tragedy—a breakdown somewhere in the normal process of growing up.

The reasons suggested are many and varied. Drugs? Alcohol? Both are undoubtedly involved at some point in far too many instances. Violence on TV and video, or on the 'big screen'? Opinions vary, though it is hard to see how the blatant presentation of sex and violence, often linked, can fail to produce a harmful influence on impressionable young minds. But would these boys and girls—for that is what they are—really slide or stray into such aggression and crime if their family and school life was what it should be? It is widely acknowledged that peer group pressure exerts a very powerful influence. Perhaps parents and teachers are just helpless victims of this modern phenomenon: the child who has been indulged and generally placed on a pedestal. Or its opposite: the child, found in every social stratum of our society, who has been neglected. This neglect is not so much in terms of providing for day-to-day temporal needs. Far more often it is a case of ignoring the child's deeper emotional needs because of preoccupation with grown-ups' affairs; of failing to see the occasional subtle but very real danger signals; even of showing open rejection.

The development of some children has been stunted because of their parents' poverty, where low income or unemployment severely limit family resources. True, appropriate benefits are available—though the freezing of child benefit has meant a net loss of income for very many. However, it is not so much those families with the very lowest incomes which suffer most. There are several forms of supplementary benefit available to them. Where income is just above the NHI level, the cut-off point for certain benefits, there is a clearly discernible 'poverty trap'.

Another widespread problem occurs where women are quite simply incapable of making any sort of weekly household budget. The limited money available may then be spent on non-essentials, or without regard to the considerable variations in price of a given article. The instinctive ability of most women to 'shop around' seems to be as difficult for those mothers as balancing the books. In the longer term the result is a chain-effect, an unhappy and eventually disastrous cycle which becomes increasingly difficult to break. One of the immediate consequences is debt, and the principal victims are the children of such families.

Quite a number of Salvation Army officers, particularly in the goodwill centres, have gained considerable expertise in the course of trying to help such women to live within their means. This adds to the woman's peace of mind as well as enhancing her self-respect. Above all, it is a useful contribution at quite a simple level to improving the quality of family life and ensuring a more helpful environment for children to grow up in.

In many different ways parents carry a very great responsibility in bringing up their children. In many instances that must include their children's unacceptable behaviour. They brought those children into the world; theirs is the primary task of nurturing them through the tender years and guiding them by example and love into adolescence and adulthood. None of us who is a parent can escape that responsibility. And if it is discharged with natural parental affection there is rarely a serious problem. Feelings of being wanted and loved are of critical importance if the word 'nurture' is to have any real meaning.

Providing a home, with food and clothing, is not sufficient in itself. The success of parenthood is not related to the ability to hand out the latest electronic toy or device on special occasions.

It has to be said that raising a family these days is far more complex and stressful for many parents than it was a generation or two ago. Trying to educate—to 'lead out from present knowledge into new areas of understanding'— is no sinecure, either. Added to that, the responsibility for helping to develop skills in relationships and employment potential demands deep insights and understanding. But for all of us, a way has to be found to break that cycle which has been referred to here. More immediately, someone has to try to help pick up the pieces where youngsters' lives have fallen apart. Among those striving to do that are

Salvation Army officers and their staff members in special centres.

Let me share some of my observations in visiting, first of all, the three community homes for children operated by the Salvation Army in Britain. Two are quite near to each other in Merseyside, the other is in South-East London. Strawberry Field, in the Woolton district of Liverpool, has had strong links with John Lennon and, since his death, his widow, Yoko Ono. As a boy, John used to play with the children here while visiting his aunt who lived nearby. At that time it was a home for girls, though later some young boys were received. As a world–class pop star, he quite often came back in later years to find peace in his 'soul-searching'. Yoko Ono has visited Strawberry Field several times, and has been generous in her moral and financial support of the work.

A few miles away, on the outskirts of Southport, I found Marshfield, another such real 'home' for some twenty children. In the Sydenham area of London is The Haven, re–opened four or five years ago following extensive rebuilding. Here there are places for thirty children. This home has been purpose–built, while the other two are large houses standing in their own grounds, which have been refurbished. The changing legislative requirements in child care, together with a desire to create maximum 'home atmosphere', have been the motivation behind this upgrading.

My main impressions? First, the quiet air of order, which still allows the children to be themselves, to live naturally. Children must play. They will be boisterous at times. The fact that they can let themselves go is evidence that they feel at home. The accommodation provides for them to live in groups of from five to ten, each in its own part of the house and with its own 'aunties and uncles', as the care staff are known. The bedrooms, washrooms and kitchen/dining area for each group have their own decor. Crockery, table-linen and similar items are of a distinctive pattern for each individual 'family'.

All that is fine, but my second impression came with overwhelming force as each officer in charge began to tell me about the individual children's backgrounds, and why they had been placed in such centres. I had the idea that such homes catered at least partly for orphans. In fact, all the children are in one form of care or another, and many of the stories are quite horrifying. I had learned of the apparently widespread practice of child sexual abuse. The media had highlighted a case involving many families in the North-East of England. But to learn what that can really mean, as one meets such children on a one-to-one basis, tends to turn one's emotions upside down.

There is a strong tradition in these homes of keeping children from one family together when they have to be taken from their parents. One story highlights the horrors experienced by some such children.

Fifteen-year-old R and her four younger siblings are in one home as a family. Their nineteen-year-old sister is elsewhere; she is an adult. R took the initiative and asked to be taken into care. The reason became clear. She had been used by her father for sexual gratification over a number of years. However, she was only his second choice, as she put it, when for any reason her older sister was not available. And all that was going on behind the windows and curtains of an apparently respectable suburban house.

So these children came into the healing atmosphere of an Army home. In the meantime, their father was charged and convicted of incest, and is now serving a prison sentence. And what of R herself? The officer having responsibility for her was quite clear: this girl, whose personality had been systematically violated, has now found a real sense of personal worth. And the younger brothers and sisters still have her with them.

At another of these homes, the dozen or so children there range in age from infancy to fourteen years. There was much the same story to tell. Child sexual abuse has become one of the main reasons for referrals. Indeed, I was told that in some parts of the country this practice was until relatively recently considered quite acceptable—just another aspect of family life. This was later confirmed in other regions I visited. Further, it is astonishing how many mothers are actively involved in this kind of abuse of children, together with fathers, older brothers and boyfriends. In two or three recent court cases which were given wide media coverage, women as well as men have been sentenced to prison for their part in organised sexual misuse of children. Much of this is closely linked to the production of pornographic literature and films.

I was told of a girl who had very recently left another of these homes, aged seventeen. For years she had regularly been used in this way by her father and two older brothers, aged nineteen and twenty-one. She then became friendly with a boy, only to find that her mother had now taken this lad for herself in a sexual relationship. Imagine her humiliation and shame when she learned that this had happened out of spite towards her rather than for physical gratification. She could have understood the latter. Those whose lives have been comparatively normal can scarcely grasp how such things can happen. Truly, one half of society doesn't know how the other half lives. And can we imagine how such children will ever overcome the emotional scars caused to those involved?

No one knows just how much child sexual abuse exists. Some social workers speak in terms of tens of thousands, while others think in six-figure numbers. Reliable estimates are virtually limited to proven cases. However, recent research points to somewhere between five and ten per cent of children—mostly girls—repeatedly being molested in this way. The true figure for isolated occurrences must be considerably higher. Some authorities suggest that as many as one in four of all girls are subject to such an act at least once during childhood. And strange though it may seem, there is often deep and abiding affection between such fathers and daughters. In many other cases, of course, it is quite different.

The allegations and revelations publicised in connection with the recent Cleveland Child Abuse enquiry are not really new. As long ago as 1907, Mrs Florence Booth wrote to a number of Salvation Army centres receiving abandoned or abused children. She was William Booth's daughter-in-law, and her husband was his father's right hand man: the Chief of the Staff, in Army terminology. In a letter which has very recently come to light after more than eighty years, she stated her intention to 'bring in a Bill against incest'. She felt that many girls 'went wrong' in their teens because of earlier sex abuse at home. She specifically asked that the officers in charge should discreetly find out details where such abuse was suspected. They were to supply her with a number of personal and intimate details which she would collate. The aim was clearly to try to amend existing, inadequate laws, and so to ensure greater protection for children in such danger.

A year later, Mrs Booth was able to inform all Salvation Army officers in Britain of the successful outcome of the thorough research and subsequent intensive parliamentary lobbying on the subject. This pressure action included the compilation of a book, *The Abandoned Child*, based on the Army's findings. This was circulated privately to 'members of Parliament, religious leaders and others interested in the welfare of children'. The revelations it contained are said to have 'caused a profound sensation' among recipients of the book—as well they might!

The main clauses of a document drafted by Bramwell Booth—Florence's husband—were eventually accepted by parliament and incorporated in the 1908 Children's Act. This piece of legislation covered a wide spectrum of child welfare concerns, of which incest was just one part. It was a notable step forward in the whole area of society's attitude towards its children and their protection.

The success achieved on this point (and by implication all the provisions of the new Act) was 'a matter of intense satisfaction to every salvationist'. This intrepid campaigner went on, 'It is safe to say that but for the efforts of the Army, the law in this respect would have remained where it had been for more than forty years.'

The advice given to officers confirmed the opinion of others who had studied this subject. 'If the Act is to be made to work, it must be done to a large extent by voluntary agencies.' Just as it was a legal obligation upon every citizen to report a crime, so it should be the responsibility of the Army and others to ensure that any children in danger of abuse should be rescued. The means by which this was to be achieved were spelled out in the document. 'Is it not as important to save a child as to punish a crime?' asked Mrs Booth.

The terms of a new Children's Bill currently being debated in parliament give rise to cautious optimism. Further protection for children is now clearly in view.

Children are placed in one of the Army's centres for reasons other than sexual abuse. Physical and emotional violence can also be psychologically damaging. Tens of thousands of youngsters suffer in this way. When parents beat or humiliate their children there is always a reason. The child may have been unwanted from birth, or may simply be different in some way from other members of the family. One lad I encountered had been the butt of his family for that very reason. He had been knocked about and humiliated in front of his two younger brothers for several years. Now he was finding new relationships in a Salvation Army home and slowly developing new attitudes.

Severe stress in one or other of the parents can cause them to 'snap' on occasion. Drunkenness is often a cause of such assaults, as is also the mental illness of a parent (very often the mother).

Placement in a community home is intended to last only as long as necessary. Re-integration into the child's natural family and home life is a primary aim, wherever possible. Where this proves to be inadvisable or even impossible, fostering may be considered. There is full and friendly collaboration between the local authority welfare personnel and the senior care staff of the home. This usually begins before referral and lasts throughout the child's stay. The child's own parents, as well as the prospective foster parents and the child himself, are involved in the negotiations.

At Marshfield, Major Veronica Stephen knows about children from areas of deprivation, where families nevertheless strive to maintain their self-respect and cohesion despite their brutalising physical surroundings—often enough there is also the brutality of a drunken husband or father. She first came into contact with the Salvation Army as a girl in just such an area of Liverpool, where she often found refuge in the local goodwill centre—just down the road from her home. She later became a Salvationist, trained as an officer, and now has both the qualifications for heading up the staff at the home, and many years of experience in social service. Like her colleagues in the other community homes, she combines a high degree of professional competence with spiritual dedication.

On a happier note, Major Stephen told me of a former girl resident who had made good. She had moved to the home counties after leaving the home, and eventually fallen in love with a steady young man. One day the phone rang in the matron's office. Would she consider providing two of the present younger girl residents as bridesmaids for the wedding? But of course! On the

appointed day the minibus headed south, loaded with a
full complement of staff and some children. Great care had
been taken with the bridesmaids' dresses and other important details. For the staff who remembered D as a small
girl coming to them in tragic circumstances, it was a great
encouragement. They had not envisaged the possibility of
one day witnessing the marriage of this poised young
woman, when they had welcomed her into their home
some years earlier.

Referring to long-term staff, there is one care worker at
Strawberry Field, now over forty years of age, who had
come there as a tot of three years. She later left to train as a
care worker, returned, and has been a member of the team
there ever since.

The children at The Haven vary in age from four to
sixteen years. Major Joyce Howlett, officer in charge,
explained that they live in three families, designated respectively 'reception', 'long-term' and 'teenage'. The first consists of children of any age whose initial placement is
envisaged to be of short duration. The second are children
who are almost certain to stay for longer; while the third
comprises youngsters in their teen years—mostly girls.
However, there are some older girls and boys in the other
two groups, and their presence and influence are usually very
helpful as older 'brothers' and 'sisters'.

Once again, sexual abuse is the main background of both
girls and boys here. In one group of eleven children no fewer
than nine had suffered in this way. But emotional and
psychological healing does take place, and despite all that has
happened to them, many of these youngsters are helped back
to self-assurance, a sense of personal value and the prospect
of living a normal life.

As in the other homes, the ratio of staff to children is
around one to two. There has to be twenty-four-hour cover,
as there would be in any normal family. Despite the need for
shift work, it is arranged that the 'auntie' or 'uncle' who puts

each child to bed (including bath-time!) is also there when they wake up in the morning.

There is a very open and natural religious atmosphere in each home. The spiritual dimension of life comes much more naturally to children than to many of their elders. The influence in each home stems far more from the example of the all-Christian staff than from any 'preaching' or religious pressure. Bedtime prayers are the almost invariable rule, involving staff and children, mostly on a one-to-one basis. Such privately shared prayers play an important part in rebuilding a child's sense of security, and in resolving the fears which tend to surface at that time of the day.

Full consideration is naturally given to any children of a non-Christian faith. In fact, these are very few. Hardly any Jewish or Muslim homes require the care which such centres provide. Their family life seems to be more stable than that of many nominally Christian families.

Attendance at Sunday school is expected, usually at the local Salvation Army corps. This requirement usually extends to the age of fourteen years. Most youngsters keenly look forward to sharing in some of the activities of the children at the corps. Contact with them is mutually helpful, as is the inclusion of some children from the neighbourhood in the play-group activities at each of the homes. Even some of the local parents get to know the mothers or fathers of the resident children; this too is a valuable experience on both sides. It certainly helps the residents to develop a sense of belonging in the community.

The Army's weekly, *Salvationist*, regularly gives news and other information about the movement's social centres. In the issue dated 4th March, 1989 were two stories concerning youngsters who have been at Strawberry Field and The Haven. Fostering is the theme of both accounts.

Coleen, aged twelve at that time, thoroughly enjoyed the local corps meetings and had expressed a strong desire to become a foster daughter with an Army family. The article invited any Salvationist parents within reasonable reach of Liverpool to make an official offer along these lines. (Coleen still had brothers and sisters at the home, and needed to keep in touch with them.)

That such an arrangement can work successfully was confirmed in the other story. Samantha was twelve when the same paper published a similar invitation in mid-1987. A resident at The Haven, she too hoped to be fostered by an Army couple, for she so much enjoyed the activities at the nearby Penge corps. A local Salvationist couple responded and today Samantha is a well-established member of the Jones family there. Such instances serve to highlight the value of a strong Christian influence in the lives of young folk when they come to the important point of leaving such a home.

Some of the older children come very naturally to a deeper awareness of spiritual values, and quite a number have become Christians. In certain circumstances this experience has to be worked through very carefully with the youngster. Consider, for instance, Mary. She had come to an Army home at the age of twelve, having been sexually abused by her father for some years. Once she came into a more mature Christian awareness of life, she had to come to terms with a threefold relationship confusion. This stemmed from the coming together in her thoughts and feelings of the differing ways in which she now regarded her father. In the first place, she was her father's daughter and she loved him in that context. We have already noted that a sexual relationship of this nature does not necessarily destroy feelings of love. Secondly, however, she was a young woman, and had experienced pleasurable sensations in the sexual act with a man, albeit her father. Subsequently, with the measure of enlightenment which came with a more objective evaluation of her life, she was aware that her father had wronged her. He had in fact broken the law. And now as a Christian she felt (without any external pressure) that she should pray for him in prison.

What a tangled skein had been woven into Mary's life! But she was sensitively and supportively helped in working through that inner maze, and has now gained considerably in self-esteem. It seems very likely that she will become a quite normal young woman. Clearly great sensitivity is required in such a situation, and plenty of time. No simplistic religious or other solutions exist. The hope of the staff is that she will one day be able to form a natural and normal relationship with a young man whom she will love, though there can never be any guarantee of that with the sort of background she has had.

In all three of these homes, the regular groups of children are augmented from time to time by others who come for short periods of respite care. These may be mentally or physically handicapped, hyperactive or simply beyond the ability of a parent or other carer to cope with. Such people need a break periodically and in this way yet another form of pressure is eased. At times life becomes almost intolerable for thousands of carers, not only of children. Attempts at suicide are not at all unknown in times of desperation. Thus each time such a child is taken in for a while, and cared for with love, someone's burden is lightened. Another positive effect is that both groups of children learn to accept each other just as they are—a very important lesson for any child to learn.

Follow-up care may continue for several years after a child has left any of these centres. Christmas and birthday cards, invitations to parties or a phone call from time to time: all help young people who want to remain in touch with those who assisted them at a crucial period in life. When children leave to join a foster family, it may be for a relatively short period, but it is usually on a semi-permanent basis. Where adoption is to be considered, the welfare authorities usually require that the child is fostered for a while—usually a minimum of two years. On the other hand, some children have been referred to one or other of these homes because an earlier fostering arrangement had broken down. No child is allowed to leave without full assurance of a secure placement elsewhere. Many of today's homeless young people have been in care, and after leaving simply drift onto the streets. The Salvation Army is aware of the risk that children who have been in care may drift into a spiral of homelessness if discharged without strong support.

Relationships with foster parents can be very good where there has been close consultation and co-operation while the child is still in the home. Major Howlett, at The Haven, emphasised that intending foster parents must come to her centre well beforehand to get to know the children. She holds it vital that such adults are aware of what they are taking on. Major Finlay at Strawberry Field also ensures that future parents come to sense the atmosphere and spirit in the home. At first they may watch the child they intend to foster from a distance—without the child knowing. Several visits may take place until all concerned are sure that the plan seems right. Of course, all the prior arrangements involve local authority child care workers. The priority given to keeping families of children together at Strawberry Field also involves foster parents after they have taken the children over. One family of six children had been received there, and later they were all fostered. Due to special circumstances only two were kept together, while the others were allotted singly to four other foster parent couples. The matron nevertheless arranged for the six youngsters to be brought together, with their new parents, on a regular basis. The local playground, birthday parties for one or other of those children, and other places or occasions are used to make sure that the children and their foster parents remain in contact with each other. In addition, the children meet their own mother once a quarter. She can never again manage them, but it is felt important that she should not lose all touch with them, nor they with her. Such planning is in addition to the management of the home with all its present child residents.

Day outings and holidays of a week or more are part of the overall programme at each of these centres, aimed at creating as natural a family spirit as possible. No effort is spared in this direction, though reasonable economy has to be exercised to ensure that costs do not escalate too much. Such homes are no cheap option for the DSS, the overall grant to each centre representing a little over £200 per child per week. Extra items, such as the recreational activities just referred to, are covered partly by fund-raising undertaken by the staff. Capital costs are, in the main, a charge on central Salvation Army funds.

From time to time various facilities are financed by local Salvation Army corps, committees of friends of a particular home, or some other body. The latter may include Rotary or other service clubs, or organisations specialising in items such as playground equipment. Local businessmen sometimes help with occasional projects.

Childhood merges almost imperceptibly into adolescence. The onset of puberty, with its physical, psychological and emotional changes, marks the beginning of adulthood. It is often a disturbing and bewildering phase in young people's lives. They may recognise that they are changing, yet not be aware of what it is all about. They feel inner turmoil, and have wild swings of mood.

Legally, adolescence ends with the coming of age. Now that young people in Britain are deemed to be adults at eighteen, it is less likely than ever that all traces of the upheavals of adolescence will have disappeared by the time adulthood is reached. Some mature much more quickly and easily than others, but for most youngsters this relatively brief phase of their lives is one of self-assertion, quite often combined with rebellion. Parental authority is challenged.

In most instances this takes the form of 'trying it on', but if parents are not sensitive to the significance of this phenomenon, the challenge hardens into open defiance and conflict. It is then father and mother who experience confusion and bewilderment: 'What is coming over our Johnny these days?' All too often this line of thinking goes on to say, 'We've done our best for him all through the years—now he treats us like this!' In fact, the adolescent is doing no more than spreading his wings or flexing his muscles in preparation for adult independence—but all the same, there are many hurts during this time.

Outside the home, the instinct to prove that one has grown up may be expressed in what is seen as arrogance, unreasonable levels of aggression and generally socially unacceptable conduct or, at the very least, disagreeable behaviour. Small wonder, then, that many youngsters come into conflict with anyone representing authority whom they encounter: parents, teachers, police.

Adolescents are still minors in law. Thus when they break the law or flout the rules by which society is organised and maintained, they have to be dealt with in a special way. Despite their often disagreeable behaviour, there has to be a great deal of patience, understanding and tolerance. Special centres are established to help such young offenders, or those at risk, to come to terms with themselves and the circumstances in which they have to live. While there are some real criminal elements in this age group, many adolescents who find themselves in difficulty with the law are 'more sinned against than sinning'. As with children's homes, such centres are now fewer in number than they were just two or three decades ago.

Reference has already been made to the two adolescent units maintained by the Salvation Army in Britain today. The House o' the Trees, in mid-Glamorgan, which served in a similar capacity (officially, an approved probation and bail hostel) for many years was closed in 1988. This was partly for reasons associated with the requirements of the Probation Service and also because of leadership difficulties.

There are nevertheless many young men who were given a new start in life there over the years. Some eventually became Christians, partly through the influence of Salvationists at the nearby Cardiff Canton corps. One such was C. Having been placed at House o' the Trees, he found the caring atmosphere in Canton very supportive during his Sunday visits there. When he had concluded his probation time, he left—and made good. He eventually married his former probation officer! Today he is himself qualified and practising in London. Now he sometimes sends clients to the Westminster Hostel (see p 133), where Major and Mrs Raybould are the officers in charge. They were formerly stationed at the House o' the Trees.

A more recently established work among adolescents in Dublin is developing remarkably. Captain Lynda Snaith and her staff conduct the programme in Lefroy House, a property acquired through a generous local legacy. The situation is ideal in that it is downtown, on the bank of the River Liffey, and near to a gathering place for many teenagers—often foot-loose and adventure-seeking. It is, however, a residential work. The need in that city is great, and the work so far has proved very promising.

On the outskirts of Kilbirnie in Ayrshire, the Redheugh Adolescent Unit receives young people who are referred from the Children's Hearings (the Scottish equivalent of the English juvenile courts) in Strathclyde.

Originally established in 1952 as a probation home and hostel, Redheugh now provides a caring programme for up to thirty-five young people of from thirteen to seventeen years of age. The professional standards are high, and the Christian motivation is seen as the secret of success. The original purchase of the house was made possible with funds from the Lipton Trust, and the work began largely through the influence of a local Salvationist who was the chief probation officer for Ayrshire at the time.

In 1971 George Steven, another Salvationist from the area, was appointed as principal warden here and remained in that position for more than fifteen years. His former deputy, Elaine Jenks, then took over in heading up the full- and part-time staff of nearly forty. This vivacious thirty-six-year old is also an active member of the Army's Kilbirnie corps, where she is the songster (choir) leader. Like George Steven, Elaine has the requisite academic and professional qualifications for the task and views her work as a vocation. She has since been appointed the Salvation Army's training officer for Scotland.

Both these gifted and dedicated Christians have given direction and purpose to the programme in line with quite frequent changes in legislation dealing with young delinquents. Such changes create considerable difficulties for those involved directly in the work, but harmonious relationships between local authorities and the staff are essential if the aims are to be achieved. These include the stabilisation of the residents and the creation of an atmosphere in which they can prepare to settle subsequently to a useful and satisfying life in the community.

There is a relaxed spirit about this place, and the use of Christian names between staff members and their charges is encouraged, though no abuse is tolerated. My first contact with Redheugh was just before Christmas 1986. The occasion was the annual dinner for almost 100 guests, mainly comprising a wide range of local personalities who give practical and moral support on a year-round basis. Following the end of this meal and some speeches (the primary reason for my presence), there was a do-it-yourself programme given by the lads and lasses then in residence. It was quite hilarious, as might be expected, and suggested to me that this was in no sense a penal institution. As soon as possible I would come back and find out more.

There is clearly a good deal of freedom within the overall programme. The youngsters are encouraged to become as independent as their backgrounds and personalities allow. The emphasis is on helping these future citizens to emerge from whatever difficulties experienced in normal development have brought them here. Apart from the cordial working relationship between the centre and the various welfare departments of the region, parents are included as far as possible. They are almost invariably invited to be present at the initial interview. There is a trial period during which both the youngster and his parent(s)—many are from one-parent families—can determine whether or not the boy or girl would really benefit from the influence and activities of the unit.

Most residents come for an initial period of from three to six months. This may be extended as needed, and in the light of experience. The average stay at present is from twelve to fifteen months, though some remain a good deal longer. Periodic reviews are conducted in consultation between the centre's leadership and the local social and education representatives. Residents who are still of school age attend a local school in which every effort is made to ensure a reasonably good integration between the ordinary student and the young person from Redheugh. Inevitably there are some tensions at times, but the positive attitude of the education authorities helps to keep these to a minimum.

An advisory group, consisting of representatives of the Salvation Army Social Services and the Strathclyde Region Social Work departments, together with local employers, councillors and various interested individuals, meets quarterly to monitor the on-going work.

The four main areas of the Redheugh programme are education, recreation, emotional development and spiritual nurture. The educational element includes the encouragement and development of domestic and social skills designed to help the resident either to return to his own family home or set up a home of his own. Handcrafts are taught, and every effort is made to prepare the youngster to gain his livelihood in satisfying employment suited to his skills. This applies equally to the smaller number of girls, whose programme will obviously be somewhat different. They need to learn housecraft and mothercraft skills if they are to become wives and mothers in the future.

The emotional and spiritual aspects of the time spent in this centre are of paramount importance. There is very often a kind of vicious circle in the family background of those referred here. The imitative process by which children can learn, can also have a very negative outworking. Older children, including some adolescents, tend instinctively to copy their elders—and when that example leaves a great deal to be desired, something must be done to interrupt the continuing cycle of unsatisfactory and unacceptable behaviour. Learning to know themselves is a vital part of the learning process in which these future citizens are involved. Understanding their own reactions, as well as the situation in which they failed to receive a stable introduction to adulthood, is essential if that cycle is to be broken and each young person's potential realised.

I learned something of what this involves when I was told about K. She came here a few years ago, having been in care elsewhere. Her mother was unmarried and her grandmother brought her up. It was when the grandmother died that K went into a home, where everything seemed to conspire against her normal development. On arrival at Redheugh she had a violent temper and her conduct was extremely aggressive. However, good teamwork by the staff gradually helped her to understand both herself and her past and future more realistically.

One of her early comments was, 'My mum's a tramp, and I don't know who my dad is.' Her mother had had a succession of 'visitors' in the house, though K characteristically refuted the allegation that she was a prostitute. Such was the 'darkness' from which K was now emerging. At school she made a good friend of another girl there and slowly settled to her new routine. At sixteen she took on a job locally, but when she was harassed (one of today's quite serious employment problems for women) she 'defended' herself. That is, she assaulted the man who had offended her. As a result she lost her job, and this led to a strong, if temporary, reaction.

However, she gradually developed a measure of poise, and later became friendly with a young man. The relationship seemed promising and the Redheugh staff who still kept in contact with her felt encouraged. When she became pregnant it seemed something of a setback—though this was just another example of the 'like-mother-like-daughter' cycle of behaviour. But K moved in with the young man and they set up home. At least this was more stable than the situation she had known in earlier years.

At about this time K learned for the very first time that her birth had been the outcome of her mother being raped. This knowledge made her think very hard, and eventually helped to restore some kind of relationship with her mother. She then moved with her partner into a local council house, and seems at present to be making a useful life for herself and her family.

Such stories could be multiplied. They vary only slightly, as observed and experienced by the staff of many of the Army's homes for young women in crisis. Elaine Jenks sees success 'not necessarily as someone who has left us and gone on to great things'. She says, 'I get a lot of pleasure in hearing from people who have simply gone on to set up a home and family.' She has recently seen one former resident become married in the little chapel within Redheugh itself. Another asked to have her baby christened there—something the staff were delighted to agree to. One man who spent a period in this centre has now been steadily employed in a local butcher's shop for twelve years, and is happily married in

Kilbirnie. There are many such causes for encouragement in what is never an easy task, yet a vital contribution to the life of the communities from which these young people come.

It would not be sufficient to stop at this point. One special aspect of Redheugh which merits comment here is the so-called 'independent unit', sometimes referred to as a 'minimum support' unit. This has been established in a refurbished outhouse situated within the twenty or so acres of the property at the centre. From the outside it still looks decidedly rustic, but the interior has been simply yet taste-fully arranged for groups of four youngsters to live in, and from which the final stage of their pre-release programme is conducted. A member of staff is on hand to give guidance when requested, but 'independence' is the name of the game. Very recently a unit for girls has been created, and this is deliberately inter-connected with the boy's unit. 'Won't you have problems here?' I asked, perhaps naively. I was gently but firmly told that there are in fact very few problems between boys and girls in this community. There may be occasional sexual activity as the residents come up to seven-teen or more years of age. However, there is a kind of group psychology at work which, I confess, intrigued me. For instance, if one girl flaunts herself in front of the boys, there is initially a 'bees-around-the-honey-pot' reaction. However, the other girls tend to take the 'enthusiast' in hand, in a gesture of mixed friendliness and warning. Further, the boys know that they have to maintain their general day-to-day relationships with all the girls, and any deviation from the accepted conventions is quickly noted—and dealt with. One result of this process is that each young person learns to accept each of the others as simply a person, irrespective of sex.

The most recent addition to the Redheugh facilities is targeted at mentally handicapped people who come in five days a week on a non-residential basis. This is quite indepen-dent of the 'probation' element, but it represents another aspect of young people learning to accept each other. In this case, it seems that the residents of the centre have created good and helpful relationships with the handicapped people who share part of their premises.

Note

1. From the Norwegian research findings of Professor Dan Olwen of Bergen University, quoted by Douglas Brown in an article 'School bullying can be cut by half', *The Times* (8th May, 1989).

5

No Place Like Home

The subject of homelessness has attracted enormous public attention in recent years. The media have revealed horrifying details. Some of these have been well documented, while others are rather melodramatic. The sobering fact is that homelessness in this country has virtually doubled in the past ten years. The problem has been most acute in London, and greatest for young single people. Agencies of various kinds are currently involved in trying to help relieve the distress caused to the genuinely homeless. The subject has become the focus of political and ideological dispute. The ethos of the two major political parties differs so widely as to make this inevitable, however unhelpful such proceedings may be in real terms. Government action affecting the situation has been severely criticised. Others point out that recent legislation has merely highlighted a malaise in society which has existed for a very long time. It is asserted that some recent adjustments to the system of social security benefits have greatly accentuated the plight of homeless people. Public opinion has been aroused, though the degree of concern is distinctly regional. In prosperous areas people generally give much less attention to this issue, which is one of the major social problems in more deprived parts of the country.

So much has been written and said that there is a good deal of uncertainty as to the true facts. One set of published statistics seems to vary enormously from another.

Statements are made which appear openly to contradict other data—opinion polls, researches and the like—which also purport to represent the situation as it really is.

One reason for this confusion is that 'homelessness' can be defined in various ways. For many ordinary, caring citizens the word conjures up a certain mental image: people who sleep out in the streets, mainly tramps, vagrants and alcoholics. For others, more closely aware of the problem, these are simply the visible homeless, a small minority of the real army of the homeless. Not all those who inhabit 'cardboard cities' are tramps and vagrants. It is true that many are alcoholics, or have some serious problem related to the abuse of alcohol or some other drug. Many more—an alarming number—are single young people aged from sixteen to twenty-three. The younger among them are particularly at risk.

The crux of the matter is that there are far too many people without anywhere they can truly call home, in a country which provides a high standard of living for most of its citizens. There is much genuine distress and despair. Many suffer a sense of complete hopelessness through no fault of their own. It is also true that some of the homeless in our midst are to some extent responsible for their own plight. Nonetheless, no one should have to live on the streets, or in derelict and insanitary buildings when two-thirds of the population live in dwellings they own.

There have always been rich and poor people in virtually every society throughout the history of the civilised world. Jesus' parable of the wealthy man who 'lived in luxury every day' (Lk 16:19) and a beggar who lay at the gate of the other's house is confirmation of that truth. Mrs Alexander reflected that fact in a well-known hymn, in which she penned the words: 'The rich man in his castle, the poor man at his gate.' Most Christians today, however, would not draw from this parable the conclusion apparently reached by the hymn-writer: 'God made them, high or lowly, and ordered their estate.' Perhaps the punctuation is important, with a comma after 'them'; God certainly created all mankind, whether high or lowly. However, it would be morally quite unacceptable to imply that he also predetermined that one should remain poor and the other rich.

The point Jesus was making emphasised the divine condemnation which falls upon those who, in their smug comfort and over-abundance of material things, allow the poor man to continue to be at their gate. And our 'gate', today as always, is in the communities where such people still languish.

It has to be acknowledged that in some respects at least, little has changed since the Victorian days of Booth's 'darkest England'. For instance, the following report by a Salvation Army officer in 1890 has a strangely contemporary ring about it:

There are still a large number of Londoners and a considerable percentage of wanderers from the country in search of work, who find themselves at nightfall destitute. These now betake themselves to the seats under the plane trees on the Embankment. Formerly they endeavoured to occupy all the seats, but the lynx-eyed Metropolitan Police declined to allow any such proceedings.

The writer had apparently spent several weeks investigating the situation on Booth's orders. This no doubt followed the latter's shock on discovering how many men and women slept under the Thames bridges. This led him to give instructions to 'do something about it'—and the first Army shelters were soon established. The situation today is little different. The dossers still know where to lay themselves down at night without being moved on by the police. Such vagrancy is still technically against the law. In passing, it is interesting to learn from the same report that the destitute of that day knew of the 'invariable kindness of the City police', and 'made tracks for that portion of the Embankment which, lying east of the Temple [the boundary of the City of London, which has its own police force] comes under the control of the Civic Fathers'. A similar form of astuteness is still discernible today among those who sleep rough, in knowing which sections of pavement have warm-air grills, or which corners of alleyways are most protected from any wind.

Any of the Salvationists and others who patrol these districts today, with blankets, sleeping bags or heat packs, as well as hot drink and food, could have written a later part of the same report, from a century ago:

> Here I found the poor wretches by the score [today on the South Bank it would be hundreds!], some men, some women, reclining in various postures, and nearly all fast asleep ... the moon ... brings into relief a pitiable spectacle. Here, on the stone abutments, which afford a slight protection from the biting wind, are scores of men lying side by side, huddled together for warmth ... some have laid down a few pieces of wastepaper, by way of taking the chill off the stones.

The writer goes on with further details which could be reported verbatim today. Perhaps one of the differences is the quite sophisticated art of securing good cardboard boxes (usually 'found' somewhere nearby) and booking one's place early to ensure a prime site for the night. Some of these cardboard shelters are fitted up with lengths of string, by means of which the occupant can open or close a carefully arranged flap. This ensures privacy as well as maximum warmth, and is really a form of closing your own front door.

In his critique of Booth's scheme, Beveridge (see pp 27-31) comments that the number of people sleeping rough in London was 'probably greater than ever before'. A census taken by the London County Council in January 1904 showed 1,797 such persons; a later count in February 1905, showed 2,181. In one night, in November 1988 a Salvation Army sponsored preliminary survey within a very limited district in Central London showed 531 such persons. A survey carried out on a cold night in April 1989 revealed 753 people sleeping rough in seventeen London boroughs. Most were young to middle-aged adults, with one woman in every seven men. These findings were issued in an interim report in July 1989 by Professor David Canter of the Department of Psychology at the University of Surrey. He commented: 'A comparison of the April survey with results from a similar but more limited pilot survey carried out by voluntary organisations, revealed almost twice as many people in areas as in previous surveys.'

Further research has shown that about 75,000 people are homeless in London. They comprise more than 18,000 in hostels of various kinds, a 'guestimate' of 30,000 in squats and about 25,000 in bed-and-breakfast hotels. The total for London as a whole is obviously much greater than it was even in the 'bad old days' a hundred years ago.

Continuing his question as to how far the Army's work among such people was 'regenerative', as distinct from being 'purely palliative', Beveridge commented sharply on 'the gratuitous distribution of meals at midnight on the Embankment or elsewhere'. He went on:

> This is not only utterly opposed to the spirit and the letter of the *Darkest England* proposals, but has been condemned by practically all competent authorities. The Vagrancy Committee in 1906 came unhesitatingly to the conclusion that both free food and free shelter were 'demoralising to the recipients and a source of danger to the community'.

It is an open question whether 'soup runs' are morally justifiable. They were revived some years ago during very cold winters. Teams from various suburban corps of the Salvation Army—such as Hoxton, Edmonton and Wood Green, Thornton Heath and others—take turns in visiting the areas in which people still sleep outdoors in winter, without any form of law enforcement to move them on.

These include the Strand, where dossers can regularly be found huddled in the doorways of prestigious employment or travel agents and other businesses. They also include parts of theatreland, Lincoln's Inn Fields and certain small parks in the West End.

How do Salvationists justify such an undertaking? Simple compassion for people who are cold and hungry? No, not just that. The provision consists of more than merely hot soup and bread. (Some generous church groups occasionally distribute fried chicken and chips!) The fact is that the Salvationist personnel have made a moral and spiritual ministry of this work. The Regent Hall corps, situated in Oxford Street, is geographically most favourably situated to link the soup run with an advice bureau and counselling centre near to all these dormitories of the destitute.

Ray Dickinson is a bandsman in this corps, but for some eighteen years he has also been responsible for their part in the rota of Army emergency soup runs. He goes out two nights a week with various helpers, and in the course of time has come to know many of the regulars. Dressed in jeans and a warm jacket, it is only his Army cap which identifies him as leader of the team. This incredibly battered piece of head-gear is used quite deliberately. Too smart a cap—let alone the normal Army uniform—might quickly spell 'authority' to people who resent any form of it. He is familiarly known to most simply as 'Cap'n', and they trust him. Major Colin Hunt and his wife, Maureen (also a major) are jointly the commanding officers of this large Salvation Army centre. They too have discovered a real spiritual ministry and are sometimes able to offer practical help to enable at least some of their 'clients' to get a foothold on the ladder back into society. Some come to their meetings on a Sunday, and a few have been genuinely converted.

The Army's well-known weekly, the *War Cry*, launched an appeal for funds to buy thousands of sleeping bags for various Salvation Army centres all over Britain. The bitterly cold weather of January 1987 gave the initial impetus to this campaign, amid media reports of dozens of homeless people dying of hypothermia. To date more than 4,500 of these bags have been given out, and every effort made to avoid fraudulent misuse of such a gesture. Thousands of blankets have been donated by well-wishers for selective and appropriate distribution. But when you come upon a man or woman genuinely shivering with cold you don't ask too many questions. Such people die almost every night on the streets of our capital city.

What happens in London is repeated in other large cities in Britain. In Glasgow, with a higher than average incidence of alcoholism, many of those sleeping on the streets and in alleyways suffer from drink-related problems. For such men, a number of whom are permanently damaged by their addiction, Captain David Arnott and his wife and other helpers provide an on-going programme of loving care, with practical aid—much as in London. Surprisingly, Captain David Tribble told me that there are few who sleep rough in central Birmingham, though his Army hostel there has its full quota of homeless people. Interestingly, the city authorities named the street in which these modern premises are situated, William Booth Lane!

In Edinburgh, the city's Council for the Single Homeless conducted a thorough survey of such persons in 1985. Salvationists were invited, with others, to co-operate as far as the Army's two hostels in the city were concerned. The Council's long-term aim is to co-ordinate the work of such centres by developing a more detailed hostels policy.

Even in such seemingly quiet and respectable places as Norwich and Bath, Army personnel have found need—and responded in characteristic manner. In both these cities Salvationists found willing and immediate help from members of various other churches. Similarly in Wrexham,

North Wales, the local Free Church Federal Council established a small, temporary night shelter for those without accommodation, through the initiative of the Salvation Army's commanding officers there. Major John Turner and his wife, Nina, have both held office in the FCFC in recent years, as area president and secretary. They saw the need and, with the Army's tradition in such matters, set about harnessing local resources of money and manpower to provide this emergency service during the winter months. From Norwich Major Eric Blake reports that some of those who had been contacted on the streets in this way accepted an invitation to attend the day centre set up at the corps not far away. Many are unemployed, and some are referred from the Citizens' Advice Bureau. A few have begun attending on Sunday morning, having sensed the spiritual motivation of those who brought them practical help at a time of great need.

Captain Philip Hendy, then in command of the Army's corps in Bath City, got together with ministers and members of various churches to set up a makeshift night shelter in the basement of the corps' premises. The local authority was fully informed, and appeared grateful that someone would do this while they were working towards the establishment of a more permanent facility. The winter of 1988–89 saw the inauguration of this work on a trial basis. Here about a dozen men (only very occasionally a woman) could find a preferable alternative to the pavements, alleys or vacant plots of land for their night's rest. Amazingly, many folk in such a situation still seem to be able to sleep deeply and soundly!

Most of these people have serious drug or alcohol-related problems. However, Hendy says that 'the root with many is that they are unwanted and unloved'.

The volunteer staff of this emergency shelter compiled an amazing record of the stories of quite a number of their 'guests'. I want to mention two of these. They represent hundreds—possibly thousands—of others with similar backgrounds.

J S, aged forty-seven, became violently angry as a young boy when he witnessed his father rape his fourteen-year-old sister. His violence led him, at the age of eighteen, to kill two people—for which he spent the next sixteen years in prison, often in a strait-jacket in padded cells. He has been on the road since his release thirteen years ago. 'Who wants to employ a murderer?' he commented. The report concludes with the simple comment: 'He is dying slowly of cancer of the spine.'

Such people are often difficult to help. They reject any thought of settling down, and even refuse hospitalisation. The Army's hostels receive quite a number of such men.

By contrast, O is twenty-three, and began taking drugs at seventeen. Three years later he lost his well-paid job in the building construction industry, having become addicted. Like many others, he had felt sure it would never come to that. For three years prior to his brief stop-over in Bath, he had been just another of the growing army of youthful drifters. Then tragedy struck when he learned that his father had committed suicide while in prison—on Christmas Eve. Imagine the effect of such news upon a person already under the destructive pressures of addiction. Deep emotions must surge, adding weight to the already heavy burden created by this foolish and ultimately disastrous habit.

One aspect—the financial side—is worthy of note here. O stated he was receiving £52.10 a fortnight from the DSS at the time. He admitted to a budget (per fortnight) which was approximately as follows: amphetamines £30, drink (alcohol) £15, cigarettes £5 and food £2.10. Clearly such an arrangement must have some hidden extras. If he is reduced to begging to help maintain his lifestyle, as he says, he can at least remain within the law. The likelihood is, however, that he will find shop-lifting or some other form of theft much easier—and more profitable.

O's story raises the question: What is the 'rich man', in this instance the average tax-paying citizen who balances his personal budget, to do about such a 'poor man' who 'lies at the gate'? 'He is there through his own folly,' we say, and few would disagree. It could be argued that he had not had an even chance in life. The fact that his father had been in prison suggests an unsettled, unstable home background. There had probably been little or no moral teaching there, and perhaps little at school. One can discuss endlessly and continue to argue the merits of the case. What is required is someone who sees the immediate need, as well as the long-term possibilities, and does something about it. A samaritan. Captain Hendy and his Christian friends and helpers were such 'first-aid' personnel. Yet even they cannot force their service upon someone who chooses to continue living as a vagrant. Maybe O will end up in a more settled place one day. Perhaps he has a few more hard and desperate experiences to pass through before he comes to his senses. It could well be that he will eventually find himself in one of the nearly fifty Salvation Army hostels and similar centres in Great Britain.

These centres are found in more than thirty cities across the country, from Inverness to Jersey, from Belfast to Blackfriars (London), from Dublin to Hull. They can accommodate around 4,000 people, most of whom have to be considered as homeless. They include both men and women whose marriages and homes have broken up. There are job-hunters who leave their families in areas of high unemployment, always hopeful of finding work in the more affluent parts of the country. Some have been released into the community from mental institutions of one kind or another, and they have no other home. An increasing number of adolescents, sixteen and seventeen years of age, are being turned out of their homes by parents, or step-parents, while others of similar age and the same degree of vulnerability can no longer live with the tensions and conflicts of their family life. They too are now part of the floodtide of rootless, homeless and often hopeless people who constitute the flotsam and jetsam of our nation.

Before going further into detail about the hidden homeless—that is, those who have no home of their own, but who are not seen on our streets at night-time—we must look a little more closely at the lives of those who still spend their nights in the great outdoors of London, even in winter. It is both sobering and salutary to learn something of their circumstances.

No one knows just how many such folk there are; certainly several thousands. That is why the Salvation Army has launched a two-year programme of research into the matter. Professor David Canter, head of the Psychology Department at the University of Surrey, has agreed to head the working party. A full-time researcher at the University, Jeanne Moore, is helping by using the most modern equipment available, together with up-to-date methods of enquiry. Personnel from the Salvation Army Social Services, led by Salvationist Tom Littler, and teams of fieldworkers from various agencies are gathering statistics and also evaluating ideas, experiences and opinions from the homeless themselves, according to the Army's *War Cry*. Littler himself was employed for some years by Manchester City Corporation as principal officer for their residential and day-care work. As a caring and concerned Salvationist, he felt he should offer to undertake this task once retired. A professional of long experience, he brings his expertise to the enterprise.

One member of the research team who is making a special contribution is Des Stockley. Studying for a doctorate of philosophy, he experienced great difficulty in finding accommodation in London. He decided to sleep out for a while, but very soon became acutely aware of the true nature of the 'alternative society of the homeless' in the capital. His very recent experience, and the insights gained, will be of particular value. The other members of the team directing this research are Jane Ball and Madeline Drake. An acknowledged expert on the subject, Madeline has written and lectured extensively, and with great distinction, on the vast and complex problem of homelessness.

Existing research is being collated with new material gathered in carefully controlled surveys. The aim, we are told, will be action; something must be done to alleviate the plight of the genuinely homeless. The information gathered will affect the Army's relief and remedial programmes, and will hopefully lead to much closer co-operation between all agencies working in this field. Major Roy Oakley, the Army's staff architect, has long been involved in concern for the homeless. Almost ten years ago he began contributing to the growing body of literature on this subject. He has been widely influential in designing new hostels, among other projects, taking into account the views expressed by residents he has encountered in his research.

But who are these people? Why do they find themselves in their present predicament? Do they really need to sleep rough, or is it in some measure their choice? Are there some criminal elements among them? Above all, how can they be helped? These were just a few of the questions in my mind during a night spent with Ray Dickinson and his colleagues of the Regent Hall soup run. It was a cold but dry evening in late January.

Once the minibus was loaded with food, blankets and other aids to keeping warm, the first stop was Euston Station. A group of regulars awaited us there at the side of the building and in the light cast from a nearby tall, modern building. The entrance to the underground car park had been closed to prevent anyone sleeping down there as they used to do. Some of these men—and one woman—seemed quite well-dressed, but were glad of a blanket to wrap around themselves in the keen wind. There were a lot of youngsters there, too; real kids, some of them. 'What are you doing here on a night like this?'

The replies were varied. 'I run away from 'ome; couldn't stand it no more.'

'Have you got a job?'

'Not ★★★ likely!' Evidently not a job-hunter!

An older man, named Tom, told me he was over seventy-three. 'Yes, I've been out here more than eighteen years, since my wife died. I couldn't seem to settle to a life of my own. But I quite enjoy it—and this winter's not been too bad so far.' He looked fit, and youthful for his age—though something in his eyes suggested a good deal of hidden strain. Had he no family? 'Yes, but I lost touch quite a while ago. When I came down to London, in fact.' A considerable number of the old hands seem to have drifted away from such ties, which were apparently none too cordial to begin with. One suspects that there are individual stories of family discord and conflict behind most of these men.

What did Tom think about his much younger companions? His reply was not very complimentary. He was a survivor, but he didn't think these youngsters would stick it for long. 'They've got no standards, and you can't trust 'em. Look at 'im!'—pointing to a lad trying to make off with two blankets. But others of the group had already taken action to stop him. There is a real sense of order in some of these communities.

During this brief stop, Mr and Mrs Christian arrived. They are responsible for the Army's much publicised midnight patrol. On this night there was little doing—but the three mainline railway termini here (Euston, King's Cross and St Pancras) are the principal arrival points in the capital for those from the Midlands and North seeking work or adventure. Young people, fresh from the provinces and unsuspecting of the dangers in a great city, are easy prey for pimps and others on the look-out for such 'soft targets'. Boys as well as girls are tragically often caught up in prostitution, as several recent television documentaries have shown.

The Army's patrol is one way of trying to prevent this traffic at source. Faith House is a small, unpretentious dwelling in Argyle Street, just a few hundred metres away. It is the base from which Mr and Mrs Christian operate. They have been honoured by the City of London, both having been made Freemen of the City in recognition of this work. Here a lad or lass can be brought for a day or two while parents are contacted, and arrangements made for son or daughter to return home. However, some object strongly to any suggestion of reunion with their families. They reject appeals to telephone home. Some have accepted a five–unit phone card. (Cards to the value of £1,500 were donated by British Telecom for just this purpose.) Others may consider using one of the advertised numbers, from which news of their present safety can be telephoned to frantic parents. The little card which is handed to these youngsters simply says: 'Left home? Send a message—no questions asked. Just give your message and we will pass it on.' Eight numbers in the major cities of Britain are then given.

Later, in Kingsway, they couldn't find the little old lady who usually sleeps outside a well-known West End theatre, long after the last playgoers have departed. Mrs Major Hunt was worried about her. So would anyone be, who cares that such people live out there. A woman of sixty to seventy years of age, sleeping on the streets, had been reported to the Army's headquarters in the City. The Regent Hall team had subsequently located her, but she was always asleep when they came. Now she had apparently disappeared. 'Let's hope she's all right. We must keep our eyes open next time.'

A lad lying on a parapet immediately above the surface of the Thames, a few yards from Cleopatra's Needle, was shivering. He was in a sleeping bag, but would be grateful for a blanket as well. 'Anything wrong, son?'

'Yeah. I've just come out of hospital. Have you got a blanket?'

One of his neighbours volunteered the information that he had been in a knife fight with another lad a few nights previously. This chap was badly cut, but had quickly discharged himself from hospital after being stitched up. He was afraid the police would get him for 'causing an affray'—perhaps even GBH (grievous bodily harm). Any thought of going into a nearby hostel was rejected out of hand. But he was feverish; how would he fare? 'I'll be all right. Just leave me alone.' He got his blanket and the team would look out for him in a couple of days.

Under the bridge at Charing Cross were quite a number of folk, though not as many as there used to be, apparently. A large area has been fenced off; yet another huge office building is being constructed. The Victoria Embankment Gardens are locked at night now. They have to be kept tidy for tourists. Some who formerly made their home here have moved to the South Bank, especially in the so-called Bull Ring under the south end of Waterloo Bridge. We later found some 200 men and women there.

Among those who were looking out for the Army van by the Embankment underground station were two young fellows, each with a girl. Propped against a convenient hoarding, they made little response to our first greeting. The girls looked about fifteen or sixteen, perhaps a little younger. Were they already in the clutches of pimps or drug pushers? More likely they had teamed up with these boys in an attempt to escape from such social parasites. One of the girls was heavily pregnant. But they were uncommunicative, and even the other folk around them seemed unable to relate to them. I tried to imagine one of my daughters in this situation. My shivering was not due to the weather at that moment. But then our girls have known the warmth and security of home and a feeling of being loved and wanted. Darkest Britain indeed!

Lincoln's Inn Fields is one of the few parks in this area not locked up at night. Even with good street lighting around the perimeter, it was not easy to locate the forms of yet more who had no roof over their heads that night. A number emerged drowsily from the bandstand building, making their way to the minibus. Many slept on—and policy is not to wake them. One chap was stretched out on a park bench, well surrounded by stout cardboard, and with his bicycle (a good one, too: I wonder where he got it?) propped in front of the seat. In this way he had two 'walls', with his coverings well secured, and himself very neatly tucked up in between. Ingenious. Would he like some soup? 'No thanks, mate; thanks all the same.'

Across the road was another group of men. One of them hailed Ray Dickinson. 'Hey, Cap'n, I got a job. Starting Monday.' In reply to Ray's question he went on, 'At Covent Garden. Sweeping up, you know.' Ray had been encouraging this man for some time. Even if it isn't what one might choose, a job is a job. And you need the money. Now, in a fortnight the man would have enough to pay the two weeks' advance rent for a room somewhere. All landlords seem to demand this now, and in a way one can understand them. Tenants staying two or three nights before 'moonlighting' represent a business loss. Yet for many that fortnight's money represents a real obstacle to getting off the streets. A single room with shared facilities can cost up to £75 a week. Poverty and vagrancy tend to be self-perpetuating.

A few words of advice, one or two practical details and a cheery 'See you on Sunday' concluded this brief but positive interlude. Any job is better than begging, as dozens (if not more) of teenagers do in London nowadays. Keith Christian of Faith House was told by a seventeen-year-old that she made £350 that way in sixteen hours. However, that is no doubt the exception.

Here I met a man I had often seen as I walked to and fro each day between the station and the office, while still working in the City. He used to sleep out, summer and winter, on a bench overlooking Queen Victoria Street. Lots of Salvationists passed him every day, and many tried to persuade him to get into a hostel, at least. One day I had sat and talked with him for a few minutes. He had been discharged from the military some years before, but had no family and no home. He quite liked the freedom of the open air. Well-spoken and unfailingly courteous, he didn't want to know about living indoors. He is evidently one of a minority who choose this way of life, though I still wonder what lies behind his bland statement. In any event, we were glad to see each other again.

As we moved on, there was a courting couple 'necking' on a bench just south of Regents Park. Funny what people will do at 2 am on a winter's morning. But there were very few women, mercifully. Many seem to find accommodation simply by moving in with a man they meet. This is at least a temporary form of shelter and security. And it's warmer tucked up in bed that way. When marriages break up—so often the beginning of a period of homelessness—women are usually left with any children, and generally manage better than men to keep a home together.

There were virtually no Black or Asian people either—at least, not in that part of London. I was told that their communities tend to look after their own people in difficulty. If that is so—and later experience in other kinds of social relief has persuaded me it is—we ought perhaps to feel ashamed. Have we, as a nominally Christian nation, at least, so far lost sight of biblical principles and teaching to the extent that we no longer care for each other? Am I not still my brother's keeper? I felt personally challenged.

Months later, I still think very often of those folk, fellow human beings who for one reason or another have lost home and family, work and economic security. Eventually they lose some part of their own self-esteem and personal dignity. It isn't easy to help some of them. Others have become case-hardened and occasionally embittered (though I found very little self-pity). A few claim to be content with their lot. I wonder! But the majority will presumably survive and make it back into a more normal life. For them, the 'cup of cold water' offered in Christ's name can make the difference between hope and despair. This is more than just a 'free distribution'; it is a spiritual ministry. On that point, I must disagree with Beveridge.

6

Home from Home

The invisible homeless, as already noted, are those who may have a roof over their heads, but who have no real home. They are far more numerous than those who sleep rough, and they represent a wide cross-section of society. We have seen that family conflict and marriage breakdown are major causes of homelessness. Alcohol or drug abuse, associated with many homeless people, is much more likely to be the consequence of one or other of those two main factors, than the direct cause.

The shadowy world of squatters is a relatively uncharted area of homelessness. The great majority seem to be men, who live in abandoned or derelict buildings. They are actually an extension of the community of street sleepers. They are often withdrawn, and do not usually want to relate to other people in the community. They represent a sub-culture, many having virtually dropped out of society.

On the other hand, the residents of a wide range of hostels form a large percentage of the overall hidden homeless population. They come to these centres for various reasons, some of which have already been mentioned. Some spend just a night or two while others find an institutionalised form of security over periods of several years. For them, such a place represents home from home. Operated by local authorities, churches, registered charities or private land-lords, hostels differ greatly in the facilities they offer and in standards of cleanliness and friendliness. Some are truly almost like home; perhaps a good deal better than the homes some residents have left. Others are simply filthy and verminous, avoided by all but the most desperately needy.

Then there are the many crisis reception centres, in addition to the bed-and-breakfast accommodation arranged by local authorities in hotels or boarding houses. These are usually intended to serve as very temporary shelter for those who unexpectedly lose their homes. The causes of such loss include default of mortgage repayments and the subsequent trauma of re-possession of property by a building society or other financial institution. A spell of sickness, job redundancy, an unexpected pregnancy, the failure of a small business—any of these eventualities may precipitate such a crisis for those whose resources are already stretched to the limit. There is scarcely any margin of safety in many of the financial arrangements entered into nowadays, in an attempt to ensure adequate housing in which to create a home. It is a perilous path which hundreds of thousands of ordinary, decent citizens nevertheless feel they have to tread.

Behind this situation is the huge shortfall in housing stock nationwide. Present estimates range up to 2,000,000 dwellings said to be necessary to resolve the housing crisis. The property boom in some regions, notably in the South-East of the country, has prevented untold numbers of people from securing a home, simply because prices are far beyond their reach. They are then obliged to resort to some other arrangement for their living accommodation, such as flat-sharing or renting 'micro-rooms', described as 'furnished,' at 'macro-rents'. This may work quite satisfactorily for some people, for a short time. As a permanent way of life it is a far from ideal solution. In other cases such 'temporary' plans drag on almost indefinitely, eventually creating family tensions or other problems, with the results already noted in terms of homelessness.

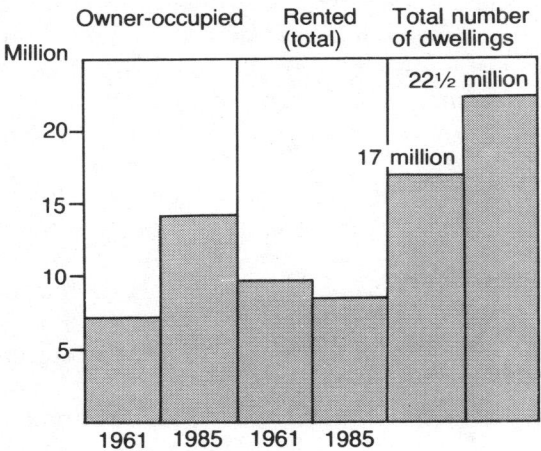

Housing stock: number of dwellings

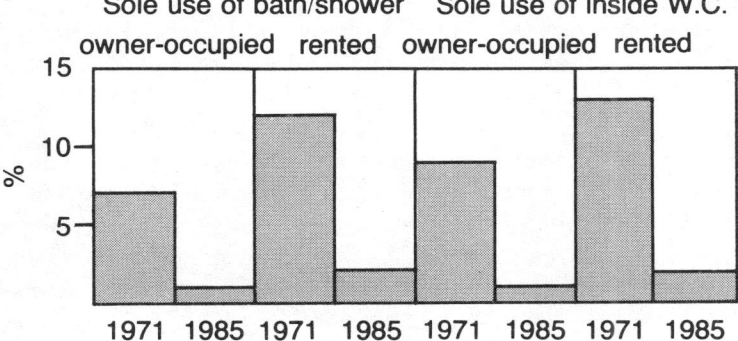

Housing amenities lacking (as a percentage of all dwellings in each category)

The government's policy of encouraging council tenants to purchase their houses or flats at discount rates is fine for those in secure employment, particularly if there are two or more incomes in the family. It was perhaps unfair that such families could formerly benefit to the extent many did, by virtue of their residence in heavily subsidised accommodation through local housing departments. On the other side of the question, this policy has also added to the dimensions of the national housing crisis. It has led to a considerable reduction in the amount of rented accommodation at affordable prices. Local authorities who sell off their housing stock in this way, either to tenants or to housing associations, are then unable to use the proceeds to build the kind of housing which is so desperately needed. Central government policy on this point makes no sense at all. Prospective first-time buyers, including many newly-weds, now find themselves in considerable difficulty and distress, if not in a total impasse, because of the free-market policies currently being pursued.

This problem is linked to that of unemployment. In the South-East and other economically advantaged regions there are more jobs on offer than applicants. In areas of high unemployment there are plenty of skilled or semi-skilled workers who would gladly avail themselves of the work available elsewhere, but they cannot afford the cost of housing in such areas. Those who leave homes and families in depressed areas, seeking employment in a region with better job prospects, often find themselves in real difficulty over accommodation. Some of them become part of the night street scene—at least, until they begin earning and find rooms. An added problem here is that prospective employers almost invariably require a permanent address—and are unlikely to accept 'The Embankment, London SW1'!

Even in new areas with exceptionally heavy demand for labour in construction projects—for instance, the Channel Tunnel—there is an element of homelessness. The workers who have come from less favoured parts of the country in search of jobs, are obliged in many instances to sleep in tents, caravans, cars or, for some, even on the streets.

The problem has been particularly highlighted in parts of Kent.

The kind of media propaganda put out by the government, which offers training for workers without jobs, to fill jobs without workers, is at best shallow and misguided. Many see it merely as a cynical way of ignoring the basic facts of life in Britain today. Exhortation to mount one's bike (or any other form of transport, come to that!) is ultimately seen by the homeless and unemployed as callous. Such flippant words from government ministers do more than simply evoke the comment, 'They don't know what they're talking about.' Coming from people with lucrative business interests and generous financial security, in addition to their government remuneration, that kind of remark is treated by very many with the contempt it deserves.

By way of example, an ordinary three-bedroomed terrace house costs in excess of £100,000 in many parts of southern Britain. In parts of the Midlands and the North, a similar property can be purchased for less than a third of that price. Rents also vary enormously, and the price boom is steadily moving further West and North. The pattern is familiar—the law of supply and demand in operation, with market forces freely at work. But when it comes down to the fundamental realities of people's livelihood and welfare, and the homes in which they are exhorted to rear their families in a return to so-called Victorian values, one may be excused a measure of scepticism. If present policies had been deliberately designed to bring this country back to an age in which prosperity and poverty became increasingly polarised, they could hardly have been more successful. Such policies, however, will do little or nothing to alleviate the real anguish and despair of millions who are unable to secure decent homes on reasonable terms.

A further significant reason for the shortage of housing

is the tremendous increase in marriage failure. Where a couple separate, there is usually a need for two homes in place of one. Added to this is the growing number of adolescents and young adults leaving intolerable home situations.

There is an almost inevitable spiral, in fact, due to rising wages in areas of labour shortage, with consequent price rises in basic commodities and services. Even within one city, such as London, the construction of luxury housing, or expensive second homes—some at seven-figure prices!—all for the obvious benefit of the well-off, excludes vast numbers of ordinary wage-earners from securing decent housing at reasonable costs.

These observations are in no sense 'sour grapes', but rather an informed commentary on the extent to which Britain is becoming 'two nations'. On the one hand people are being actively encouraged to become property owners, share-holders and credit card users. On the other, a very large number are being continually frustrated in their efforts to better themselves, because there are insufficient checks and balances to prevent the growing gap between the prospering and the struggling. At the root of much of that situation is the instability caused by homelessness.

Most people in this country manage to secure and maintain reasonable accommodation for themselves and their families. Even there one has to add 'at considerable cost'. When a mother feels it imperative to go out to work full time in order to help cover mortgage costs, there is a price to pay. She is often under extra stress as a result of trying to fulfil this double role, particularly when the children are younger. The number of latch-key clubs is growing, in an attempt to prevent children from roaming the streets before and after school, while both parents (if there are two) are at work. Certainly greater consideration must be given to the substantial minority for whom home ownership is not possible.

The generation of national wealth has a vital part to play in improving the general well-being of society, but that wealth must be much more evenly distributed than it is at present. The underlying Christian ethos of mutual responsibility and solidarity is rapidly being eroded. The emphasis is so strongly upon material acquisition and possession that few can resist its magnetism. One off-shoot of this trend is the enormous growth in consumer credit debt. The total owed by customers of just eight major High Street stores which issue their own credit cards has now risen to well over £1.1bn, according to the Retail Credit Group. The average amount owed for each credit card is in excess of £150. Total consumer credit is estimated at £36bn.

The Women's National Commission says that the end result of easy credit is often divorce and lost homes. A report commissioned by the Social Security Advisory Committee was reviewed by Jill Sherman in an article 'Credit, Debt and Poverty' in *The Times* (3rd March, 1989). The article pointed out that an estimated 2,000,000 households are in debt by up to £10,000, excluding mortgages. Some face debts of £50,000 or more. Loans to private households doubled between 1980 and 1987. Half of families in debt are unemployed, but wanting their 'share of the cake'. The majority of those with debts are in the lower income brackets. Around 200,000 families have multiple debts. The high rates of interest charged by some stores has become a national scandal. The astronomical rates charged by 'loan-sharks', often exorted under considerable duress, are both immoral and criminal. The Salvation Army is only one among a number of major bodies which have called upon the government for much stricter controls on instant credit and interest rates.

It is righteousness, not riches, which exalts a nation (see Proverbs 14:34) and there is nothing very exalting or edifying in the present inequalities. Indeed, they are distinctly *un*righteous. One can only hope that history will not return a verdict of 'guilty', on a charge that our generation gained the world and lost its soul.

Many have raised their voices in criticism of these (and other) government policies and will surely continue to do so. Church leaders, academics and professionals from many walks of life, as well as opposition politicians, have left the government in no doubt as to their concern for the predictable consequences. Regrettably, the main reaction so far has been irritation and annoyance—as though such public-minded people had no business interfering in these fundamentally important matters. Alternative proposals have been put forward, and we must wait to see what effect they may have in the longer term.

In the meantime, this is another of those aspects of life in Britain today in which the paramount need is for someone to do something in immediate and practical terms. Something to help the homeless in their deprivation. Something to help restore to them a sense of worth and value as citizens. Among those engaged in such work, as one would expect, is the Salvation Army. Salvationists are endeavouring to maximise the effectiveness of their resources and the movement's infra-structure of premises, programmes and Christian principles in favour of such unfortunates.

We have already taken a general look at the Army's network of hostels and other centres for homeless persons. I have been privileged to visit more than half of these in recent years, a dozen of them during the past few months. The work undertaken in such places requires a high level of motivation and commitment. It often tests the tolerance and temper of the care staff, but because they see it as a caring, spiritual ministry they find the needed grace and love. The key concepts, if not always articulated in such words, are reclamation, restoration and rehabilitation. Eventual resettlement is seen as the ultimate goal in the rehabilitative process, whenever possible. So let us look into this other world, in which contemporary servants of Jesus Christ are involved in modern miracles.

The two largest of these centres are also among the oldest, and both are in central London. Many new buildings have been erected for the Army's Social Services in recent years to replace out-dated premises. In a few instances the old structures had become dangerous and had thus been condemned. But the Westminster and Blackfriars hostels have survived. In itself that says something significant. It infers that there has been a continuity of operation for many decades—meaning that every night between 200 and 300 homeless men have found refuge in each. In real emergencies those figures can be extended a little. The staff nevertheless have to observe the conditions set by the public authorities, which are much more stringent than in William Booth's day—thankfully. No one wants to see a return to Victorian conditions. On the other hand, it is hard to have to say, 'Sorry, we're full,' when urgent telephone calls are received from social workers or other welfare personnel on behalf of someone in real need of accommodation. And that happens more often than the officers in charge would wish.

Major Brian Raybould, in charge of the Westminster Hostel, is one of the Army's more unorthodox officers, and perhaps one of the most caring. He epitomises the slogan 'With heart to God and hand to man', sometimes used in connection with Salvation Army social work. A slightly built man, Raybould has his feet—and his mind—solidly on the ground. He knows the thoughts and feelings of his men in an earthy yet profound way. He knows their language, too. Most people would find conversation with some of these men difficult, if not impossible. Raybould greets them naturally, passes the time of day with them, and counsels them—all in their own idioms.

Some would find his language rather too colourful at

times—but he communicates! 'Talking is great therapy for the men,' he observes. And of course he's right. When someone stops to talk and to listen to you, you feel you're being treated like a human being. And that is not an everyday experience for such folk. That principle goes for all the Army's officers working in such centres.

Raybould would be the first to acknowledge his dependence not only on God, but on his wife, Kay. As with all such Army couples, both are officers and they work as partners. If he occasionally tends towards going over the top she gently brings him back to earth.

In 1910, the novelist H Rider Haggard published a book entitled *Regeneration*. The sub-title clarified its contents: 'Being an account of the Social Work of The Salvation Army in Great Britain.' This keen supporter of William Booth's land colony plans now described visits he made to a number of hostels and other social homes functioning at that time. He began his report on the Great Peter Street (Westminster) centre thus: 'This fine building is the most up-to-date men's shelter that The Salvation Army possesses in London.' Today the outer structure remains solid and quite impressive to the eye, though the interior has had to be extensively renovated. Haggard continued: 'I visited it about eight o'clock in the evening, and at its entrance was confronted with the word "Full", inscribed in chalk upon its portals, at which poor tramps, deprived of their hope of a night's lodging, were staring disconsolately.'

And that was at a time when, as Haggard recorded, the hostel was 'wonderfully equipped [with] . . . huge dormitories capable of accommodating about 600 sleepers'! The difference in principle between then and now is probably to be found in the distinction between a shelter, pure and simple, and a hostel where certain facilities and activities may be found which do not exist in a 'dosshouse'.

What kind of men fill this place nowadays, when

accommodation has been reduced to not much more than a third of its capacity at the beginning of this century? Who are the residents of this former billiard ball factory? 'The majority seem to need life-long care somewhere. Many were in care already as children,' says Raybould. 'We try to see each man at least once a month for a proper interview. Sometimes they swear appallingly, even in the presence of my wife!' But Mrs Raybould is quite used to that, and they both see such behaviour as an expression of otherwise intolerable feelings of aggression. Very many have drink-related problems. The majority originate from one or other of the inner London boroughs. Some are mentally ill, or handicapped. A recent survey in the larger London hostels indicates that around one-third of residents were suffering from schizophrenia. Almost half the Westminster centre population are on regular medication of some kind. Many of them are spill-outs from psychiatric wards which have closed due to government policy. They are not considered dangerous, nor do the police usually prosecute them for minor offences. They are known, and the police keep in touch with the hostel staff. The basic fact, however, is that they have no other home than this.

For example, G had a mental age of five when he came, despite his exceptional physique. The police brought him, and he is still in trouble from time to time for acts of public indecency. He urinates in the street. For a long time he has called out after female passers-by. Some fear him, but he is not at all violent. 'Do you know Mary P?' was often his question to such women. Psychiatric investigation, and regular little chats with the staff, eventually revealed that this had in fact been his mother's name. She had abandoned him at the age of seven. Ever since, with his mental and emotional limitations, he has been seeking her. Now, with compassionate understanding and care, he has attained a mental age of eight. Limited though it be, that is progress. Some light has come into his darkness.

R is older. At sixty-two, he is a tiny man, with some very strange behavioural patterns. He can be seen washing his hands in street puddles. Quite often he goes out in the morning to sweep the street outside—with his own broom. Evidently the municipality's standards are not up to his. He sometimes climbs into the huge rubbish containers situated outside nearby apartment buildings, re-arranging the contents. When a shower of refuse comes rattling down the chute, he calls out, 'Thank you.' Yet when he goes out a little later, quite oblivious to what is happening in the Houses of Parliament just around the corner (let alone in Westminster Abbey), he buys *The Times* and *Guardian* in order to do the main crossword puzzles. He usually completes very quickly what others—the more 'normal'—pore over for hours. Occasionally he will ask Raybould about a certain clue, to which the latter replies, characteristically, 'I haven't a clue, R.' But he will stop and discuss the point with him.

As an extension of their caring concern for those down on their luck or incapacitated in some way, the Rayb+oulds go around the district from time to time. Not an official patrol—just a divinely guided wander. They look for anyone who seems to be in special need. Mrs Raybould smiles as she relates an incident involving a local prostitute, whom she had come to know quite well. At thirty-six this woman was considering retiring from the game. One day, in all seriousness, she offered the woman Salvationist her patch. It was outside a West End hotel, near the main entrance, and had the special benefit of a warm-air grille in the pavement: it gets pretty cold standing there in winter, waiting for 'custom'.

Far from being offended or overly amused, Mrs Raybould saw that the woman was in fact offering her her most valuable asset. It is this sensitivity of outlook and insight which enables Army officers such as the Rayboulds to minister spiritually to these folk, as well as offering them shelter and food.

'Do you have a problem with drugs?' I asked. In reply Raybould told me of a day when he had been standing just inside the hostel's entrance, when three well-dressed men came in. They looked out of place there. The Major was about to ask them what they wanted when one of them spotted him. 'My God, it's you, Cap'n,' said one, and they all fled. In that moment Raybould recognised them. All three were well-known drug pushers in the Notting Hill area where the Rayboulds had earlier worked for ten years. 'I hate to think what might have happened if they had got a foothold in here,' he said.

I asked one final question: 'You have what is by modern standards a very large hostel. Many would crticise the Army for continuing to harbour so many men under one roof. Is there still a place for such centres today?'

'Yes, in certain circumstances,' replied Raybould. 'These places are part of an essential safety net in society, even if it's temporary. But we need further progress in buildings, facilities and programmes. But there's still a need for hostels, at least around here.'

The spiritual welfare of the residents is covered partly by personal contacts with each and partly through the regular gospel meeting held in the centre. This is the pattern in all such Army centres. Attendance is voluntary, of course, as is participation in public meetings in nearby Army corps. There are strong links between the Westminster Hostel and the Regent Hall corps, in Oxford Street.

One man, who eventually became converted, according to the light that was in him (an important proviso to make in some instances), later testified to the fact that he had 'exchanged the bottle for the keys of the kingdom'! When last heard of he was still 'dry' and doing well. He is one of a surprising number who experience a genuine change of heart, leading to a quite new lifestyle.

Less than two miles away, on the south side of the Thames, stands the well-known Blackfriars Hostel. The

Army acquired this building in 1891 from a temperance society, and adapted some stables at the rear to increase the accommodation. For some time this was as high as 800 places, though that figure was reduced to 550 in 1895. Rider Haggard records the information given him at the time of his visit in 1910 concerning the character of this centre. It was seen as 'the dredger for, and the feeder of, all The Salvation Army's Social Institutions for men in London'. He likened it to 'a dragnet set to catch male unfortunates in this part of the metropolis'. He especially commented on the cleanliness of the entire premises, with floors constantly scrubbed and all bunks disinfected once a week. Vermin were unknown, making this the exception among common lodging houses of that day.

A great variety of men still come here nowadays, where Major David Moffat and his wife, Eileen, are responsible. In a number of respects, the population and purpose is the same as at Westminster. The building is really quite inadequate to fulfil this role in the context of the contemporary social work policy. Yet this place, too, serves as a vital safety net for those in danger of falling beyond help and hope.

Moffat's own story is of particular interest, and helps him to understand the background of those who seek accommodation here. He grew up in South America, where his parents were church missionaries, and completed his schooling in the USA. Due to a misdemeanour he was expelled, first from the school, then from the country itself. He lived in Canada for some years, joining the military before having to leave that country too. His ship eventually docked at Southampton, and he subsequently arrived at Waterloo Station, London. From there he made for a place which had been recommended to him, just down the road—Blackfriars Hostel!

In retrospect, he confesses to feelings of 'utter despair' as he entered the premises. It all seemed so depressing and run down, especially for a young and active adventurer, fresh from the New World. He stayed just two nights, but through a chain of events he steadied up and eventually became a Salvationist. After a period of training he was commissioned as an officer, which led to a series of appointments in the Army's Social Services in Britain. Then, nearly thirty years later, he took charge of the very hostel in which he had found temporary shelter as a homeless person. He tells now of a similar sense of despair as he walked in to view his new area of responsibility. Little had changed over the years. Indeed, little can be done in terms of structural alterations—yet the need for this haven of refuge never diminishes. And Moffat has seen some small but significant material improvements. He and his wife also have the resources of divine grace to help them in their 'nearly impossible task': Beveridge's assessment of such work in Booth's day.

Above all, he understands the thoughts and feelings of the present occupants, having been there himself. Thus he can respond compassionately to their deeper needs.

There is an acute need for some form of therapeutic work within the centre's programme. It is all very well to have regular visits by community psychiatric nurses and occupational therapists. Their professional skills and continuing availability are indispensable and greatly appreciated. The voluntary contribution made by a number of part-time associate workers and consultants is highly valued. However, the younger men, at least, urgently need something to do. Most have no employment. Quite a number are ex-servicemen who have so far failed to re-adapt to civilian life. The British Legion as well as the Soldiers', Sailors' and Airmen's Families Association are very helpful here. The real need, however, is for workshops where men can improve their skills and so work towards eventual reinsertion into society.

The trouble is that the premises simply do not lend

themselves in any very practical way to such adaptation. Nevertheless, a small place has been fitted out, and the experiment has proved successful. At least ten men can benefit at any one time from the kindly oversight of a couple of instructors. Furniture renovation, picture and mirror framing, basket-making and some straightforward printing work are the principal activities.

In some cases it takes time to motivate a man to work, especially if he has been without home or work for a longer period. The staff see this as part of the rehabilitation process. Some men have lost the will to improve themselves. Those who are still enslaved by drink are particularly prone to a sense of despair and hopelessness. They need encouragement to have a go. The fact that both instructors I met had themselves come through to sobriety and industry in such a centre helps to establish a creative rapport.

It is a small yet hopeful beginning. It is a policy trend also being worked out slowly in a number of other Army hostels in this country, where old buildings have frustrated past efforts at such a development of the care programme.

A variety of men live in Blackfriars Hostel. Some thirty have mental problems, while a similar number are frail, elderly pensioners. There are generally from seventy to eighty who stay only a short while; most are unemployed and move around looking for work. Between thirty and forty have been here for a long time, some for several years. In the main they are not capable of making the transition to a more normal life. Quite a high percentage of the overall population are homeless and unemployed. A social skills course is available for such men, in which budgeting, cooking and general homecraft are covered. Relationships, securing a job and wise use of leisure time are further aspects of this programme, which is part of the overall emphasis on resettlement. Even some of the older residents are eventually rehoused in co-operation with the local authority. During the eighteen months to the end of 1988, no fewer than forty-two men were able to begin a new life this way. A little more than half that number were able to set up homes of their own, while the rest went to 'group homes' or places of more permanent residence for otherwise homeless people.

Of those who remain at Blackfriars, a number are employed in simple domestic tasks within the limits of their competence: kitchen work, cleaning, etc.

A bail unit operates here too, even though it is not yet officially recognised by the Home Office. Negotiations to this end are in progress. Pending trial, young alleged offenders are released on bail provided they can give a fixed address. The centre provides for that possibility. The idea was pioneered at Booth House, in London's Whitechapel Road, and has now been taken up by the probation service.

One of the more innovative schemes within the Army's social operations is known simply as the 259 Scheme (the figure refers to the street number in Waterloo Road, at the rear of the premises). It is a resettlement scheme, designed for young men from sixteen to twenty-five years of age. Up to twelve lads at a time can be received, many of them alienated from their families. When I visited this significant unit, Dr Nim Njuguna was in charge. A Kenyan who came to Britain to study, he worked on a similar scheme in Scotland after graduating. 'It was too humanistic,' he says, as a Christian, 'so I came here.' He has since moved on, but the work continues.

Some of these young residents come from the main part of Blackfriars Hostel, while others arrive from a variety of agencies or other hostels. The aim of the programme is 'to assist the residents in gaining better control over their lives by developing a deeper understanding of their past experiences, by increasing their self-confidence and self-esteem, and by developing their emotional and practical skills for successful independent living'.

They begin with a four-week evaluation phase to test their suitability and motivation. Once this is determined they remain for a further period of from three to twelve months. Their programme covers both emotional and practical needs, and maximum support is aimed at through the key-worker system. This involves each of their staff of five full-time and four part-time workers being allocated certain participants, to whom they will relate throughout the course. Regular and frequent reviews are held involving each resident and his key-worker. Where continuation is felt to be inappropriate, every assistance is offered in finding alternative accommodation. There is quite a high turnover rate; not all such men can stay the course.

A final phase of 'visualisation' is then entered, in which the local authority provides accommodation in the district for those who are ready to move on. That can be quite a quantum leap for anyone who has not had responsibility for himself and his pattern of living. The Young Single Homeless Section of Southwark Borough's Housing Department has proved very helpful in this respect, though their resources are limited. The unit maintains a watching brief, giving any support needed and offering follow-up encouragement.

The scheme also envisages the possibility of receiving young prisoners. They will be seen six months before release, and later spend the final weekend of their sentence in the unit. This will demonstrate their willingness to benefit from the experience, and their suitability for the course.

Where there has been a rupture in family relationships, the 259 Scheme staff encourage the young man to seek reconciliation. Advice and guidance are offered, though staff members do not enter directly into such negotiations.

While this programme operates in a largely autonomous way, it is nevertheless a part of the overall responsibility which Major and Mrs Moffat carry. They bring their own spiritual influence and pastoral concern into the life of the unit and seem well accepted by the young trainees.

The concept of resettlement, as perceived by Salvation Army personnel engaged in such work, is fourfold. First, training is provided for hostel residents to help them acquire the skills needed for independent living in the community. Secondly, such people need much encouragement in order that they may realise their maximum potential once re-settled. Thirdly, adequate arrangements must be made for housing them; resettlement can only occur where such provision is made. In practice, hostel staff negotiate with local authority housing departments, housing associations and (occasionally) private landlords. Finally, follow-up contact with persons resettled must be available as required or desired.

The above account of the provisions made for homeless people has focused on the London area. This is clearly where the major concentration of homelessness is to be found and, as indicated, the two hostels referred to have the largest capacity to receive such people. However, similar facilities are available in other hostels in the capital, and a range of programmes is operating in centres in many provincial cities. It is not possible here to refer in detail to each of these, though the work undertaken in them matches that of the larger centres both in the quality of care and the degree of professional social work. Just a few typical examples must suffice.

A number of these places are housed in fairly modern, often purpose-built premises. The Booth House complex in London's Whitechapel district might be described as 'the flagship' of such centres of Christian care. Named after the Army's founder, it is situated quite near to the spot where William Booth commenced an open-air ministry which was to become the genesis of the Salvation Army. The present complex was erected in connection with the 'For God's sake, care!' appeal, at the time of the movement's centenary celebrations in 1965.

Booth House includes hostel accommodation for 170, many of whom must be defined as homeless. There is also a separate eventide home within the complex, which is home to nearly forty elderly men. This subject will be developed further in Chapter 8. The detoxification unit here is one of three operated by the Army in the United Kingdom, which in turn are linked to several other centres catering for victims of alcoholism (see Chapter 7).

A number of the hostels nationwide each have accommodation for more than 100 people: Glasgow (two), Belfast, Cardiff . . . the list extends to some sixteen cities. In London, the Hopetown Centre caters for just over 100 women in three categories. Approximately one-third of the total are elderly and tend to be long-stay residents. Another third are defined as 'low support mentally ill', while the remainder are 'direct access' guests. Most of the latter are unemployed. A considerable number have suffered marriage failures, with alcohol abuse often at the root of this pattern of breakdown. Quite a few of the women in each of these groupings have behavioural problems, yet all can find here an ambience of quietness, and spiritual and emotional support. Most have been deprived of normal family life and suffer from insecurity and anxiety. They are quite often withdrawn in the company of others.

All the women are accommodated in pleasant single rooms in a very agreeable situation—despite the proximity of the nearby busy Whitechapel Road. Major Catherine Johnstone, officer in charge of this centre, told me that a high percentage are in familiar surroundings here in the East End of London. She also emphasised that the qualified care staff try to foster a spirit of independence, whilst enhancing the ladies' social relationships. They know the therapeutic value of physical touch, representing acceptance. Just being there and being willing to listen are highly important aspects of the care programme. They also provide any needed medication, therapy and general body care.

Most of the residents receive income support of a little over £80 per week whilst in the centre. Of this, £70 will be paid for full board. If preferred, the bed-and-breakfast rate is £49 weekly. There are no limits on age or length of stay. There is rarely a vacancy, and applications always exceed the number of available rooms.

The seven other Army centres catering exclusively for women are smaller. In Edinburgh, the Vennel Hostel can receive fifty-five ladies. It is situated near the centre of the city, not far from the Pleasance Centre for men, which has accommodation for more than eighty.

The needs of Northern Ireland may be less than in many of the great industrial regions of England and Scotland, yet here, amid the continuing sectarian conflict, Centenary House in Belfast is home to 110 men. Although it is a more recent building, there is already need for refurbishment to meet changing conditions and requirements. A considerable amount of capital investment is being made and there are hopes of an eventual extension.

Tom and Audrey McAuley are in charge here. They are local Salvationists, and have been in the business world for most of their married life. More recently they have supported previous officers in charge. Their spirit of dedication, combined with their managerial skills and business acumen, persuaded the leadership that they would be ideal to direct the work.

Tom wanted me to meet some of his men, so we went first to Willy's fiftieth birthday party. He lives in the wing set aside for the frail elderly and mentally weak. And what a fascinating group they proved to be! Ten of them, all enjoying the treats organised by a group of the younger care assistants. Willy told me that he had never had a birthday party in his life. It is quite possible, of course. An astonishing number of people appear to have been deprived of what most of us take for granted. On the other hand, memory may have faded. Certainly some of his friends told me, smilingly, not to take too much notice when he informed me—very confidentially, but in a loud voice!—that he was going to live in a flat elsewhere in Belfast. Alas, he is one of the many who could not reasonably fend for themselves, and would probably be homeless if this place did not exist.

Such people spend their days wandering around the city area, though not too far from base: the shops, the park and particularly the library. No one can be sure how many people in Britain suffer from such mental problems as schizophrenia, Alzheimer's disease or other manifestations of senility. In Centenary House, as in several of the other Salvation Army centres which house such people, social and domestic skills are taught for the benefit of those who show potential for resettlement.

I found Rita interesting to listen to. She too is a Belfast Salvationist, who has worked here for more than ten years. She can remember when things were not as good as they are today. Her critical views about the past are well tempered with appreciation for all that is now done to 'improve the quality of life for the residents', to quote from the stated aims of all Army homes of this kind.

Before concluding this all too brief survey of Salvation Army facilities for the homeless, some mention must be made of the highly significant contribution made by the Army's housing associations. The smaller of the two operates in Scotland along the same lines and with the same aims as the Salvation Army Housing Association Ltd based in London. There are at present no projects in Wales and the association cannot operate in Northern Ireland.

Each is defined as 'a free standing and independent body controlled by a management committee comprised of senior Salvation Army officers and lay persons with housing knowledge'. Government grants and loans are available to these enterprises, which often use the Army's Social Services as agents who provide management services and staffing. They also administer a number of housing complexes independently.

Describing the associations as being 'concerned for the housing and welfare of homeless persons, the elderly, and those earning a low wage', the report of the committee of management then defines its aims: 'Our provision [of housing] must be at rents which the normal hourly paid worker can afford, given the usual assistance of Housing Benefit.' The statement continues by expressing concern lest 'the poverty trap whereby our tenants are dissuaded from seeking employment due to high rent levels' is widened.

As at mid-1989, the association covering projects in England has become responsible for the construction of thirty centres. These include hostels for men and women with places for over 1,200, sheltered housing for some 140 elderly persons, and flats for almost 100 single people, women and children in crisis and retired Salvation Army officers.

One of the best of the SAHA-sponsored multi-programme centres is the Tom Raine Court complex in Darlington. First, there is a thirty-four-bed hostel, named after a long-serving and highly respected local Salvationist. This is a replacement for the old building, which had reached the end of its useful life as a home-from-home for homeless, unemployed and other deprived people. There is the now familiar mix of alcoholics, mentally ill and elderly, housed in separate wings of the building. Adjacent are twenty-six single flats.

Major and Mrs John Luce head the very competent staff team here. Their responsibilities cover the oversight of the hostel, with its various programmes, and the flats. Two of these are equipped for physically handicapped people—as is now the pattern in other such projects. By way of example, one of the present (1989) residents in such a flat is a qualified chartered accountant. Following a serious road accident he was paralysed and thus confined to a wheelchair. He lost his girlfriend at that time and his family proved over-protective. In his frustration he wanted above all to become independent again, and his present accommodation is proving to be a big step in that direction. Both physical and emotional therapy are available within the complex for such people. Regular meetings are held with tenants of the flats to discuss any problems or suggestions which may arise. Such dwellings represent an important step towards independence for otherwise homeless people. They also provide the needed accommodation for the first phase of resettlement—particularly for some physically or mentally disabled persons.

There have been fewer homeless men in this hostel than elsewhere. Most were women, temporarily stranded in the city. By contrast, there is a considerable number of mentally ill, for whom an excellent rehabilitation programme operates. Some of the activities are held in one or other of the large rooms comprising the purpose-built community centre. A workshop equipped with tools for various kinds of craftwork functions under expert supervision, and various games also have an important role in the programme.

The community centre premises are available at times for the use of other groups in the town. Seminars run by the local authority social services; luncheon meetings for a large group of people involved in mental health work; and a 'loss and bereavement' course established by a local counselling group, are some of the additional activities undertaken in this fine new building.

In all this there is a close and cordial working relationship between the staff of the complex, the local Salvation Army corps, the housing association and a wide range of local professional people concerned with the many aspects of the care programmes. Again, full emphasis is given to the spiritual welfare of residents. Short daily prayers are attended by between twenty-five and thirty staff and residents, and in addition quite a number enjoy bright Sunday meetings. Personal contacts and on-going counselling are a vital part of the ministry of the officers in charge.

More than 200 miles to the south, in the town of Swindon, is another multi-programme centre, sponsored and built by the SAHA. Davis House has 114 places for men and women. It is a somewhat up-market form of hostel, like Darlington and several others. Captain Richard Cook who, with his wife Pauline, is in charge acknowledges: 'This kind of centre leaves out a whole stratum of society.' He points out, however, that this is inevitable in view of the rather more specialised work undertaken. The needs of other categories of people in difficulty are catered for by other agencies and Army centres elsewhere.

One of the strong emphases here is on the problems of alcoholics, both men and women. Cook and some of his staff work closely with Gloucester House, an Army alcoholism rehabilitation centre in the nearby village of Highworth. They also maintain links with local agencies and institutions working in this field. (See Chapter 7 for an outline of Salvation Army services for victims of alcoholism.) In this work, the Captain is particularly well able to understand the situation in which those who abuse alcohol find themselves. He is one of several Salvation Army officers who have come through from such problems themselves, to involve themselves in the treatment and care of others.

The population of Davis House is a closely-knit community. Rather than reserving separate parts of the premises for the different categories of residents, Cook has opted to mix them freely. This seems to work well, though all have their own rooms to retreat to. Apart from the frail elderly, the mentally ill and the alcoholics, there are families in crisis, women with special pre- or post-natal needs and single mothers. Young single homeless men also find at least temporary refuge here.

The influence of stable family life is emphasised by the very visible presence of both Richard and Pauline Cook and their three sons. The residents watch the interaction and general relationships of this family with considerable interest. They see Mrs Cook's role as a mother-figure in the complex as having great importance. Indeed, this is true in virtually all such Army centres.

Among the care staff is Mark—he is in fact the Marquis St Leger, of the well-known French-Irish family. He has his own small office on the premises where he receives a case-load of thirty or more people. Most of them are referred to the centre from elsewhere. His own tragic experience in life helps him to identify with others in deep emotional distress. 'My own church could not help me in my bereavement' (he lost his wife and two daughters in a car accident), 'but after gaining the CQSW qualification I came here.' He knows of the divine inner strength which is available in times of human extremity, and is a valued member of the social counselling team.

One of his aims is 'to break the circle of residence and freedom'; that is, of resettlement, relapse and renewed residence. He is concerned that too many people prove incapable of caring adequately for themselves when resettled. They tend to revert to their old ways and eventually need to come back into residence in a centre such as this. That represents a considerable setback for the individual concerned, and a certain failure in the programme.

The mentally weak or ill constitute a significant part of the homeless population here. A number are accepted after careful consultation and close collaboration with the staff in psychiatric wards or clinics. Others just drift in, having slipped through the net where less care is shown at the time of closure of such places. The Salvation Army has made strong representation on this subject, in particular to Lord Nottistone, sponsor of the Schizophrenia Aftercare Bill. Colonel Sidney Gauntlett, a Salvation Army doctor, referred to the many people in the Army's hostels who suffer from this form of mental illness: up to one-third of all residents. The Colonel wrote, 'Many of these people had treatment in the past, and because there was no adequate after-care and medical supervision, they relapsed in their illness without anyone being aware of what was happening.' And he should know, after a number of years as medical adviser, then chief secretary, within the movement's Social Services throughout the United Kingdom.

The causes of such illnesses are obviously varied. However, Mark gave his opinion to the effect that poor family background and long-term unemployment are major contributory factors. There are many, of course, whose mental problems are hereditary. Some experience great frustration if they are over-protected. They then quite often engage in anti-social behaviour as a form of protest against their lack of independence. Some display strong anti-authoritarian attitudes. Most are on medication, which is naturally available here. Occasionally Mark or one of his colleagues may be threatened by a psychopath. Certainly this is no easy task, nor are there any simple solutions to the plight of very many who pass through this centre—which is nevertheless home to them.

The SAHA has provided forty-five flats in central Nottingham for single homeless people. This facility is managed by the Army's Social Services. A similar project is nearing completion in Swindon, providing thirty flats. Further projects of this character are planned for Ancoats (Manchester) and Newbury.

One other significant housing association project must

find a place in this record. This time it is the association which administers the whole programme; the Army's Social Services are not involved. In conjunction with the town council of Clacton-on-Sea, the SAHA has funded, constructed and furnished nine three-bedroom houses in the district. These provide comfortable temporary accommodation for homeless families who would otherwise have been placed in bed-and-breakfast accommodation.

The Project Co-ordinator, resident on the site, is Mrs Jean Wright. She is an active Salvationist in the local corps, and brings to this assignment her well-developed sense of order in addition to the empathy which is so valuable an asset in her working relationships. Jean and her husband, Tom, see this as a way of helping people who gratefully accept this haven in a storm at a time of personal and family crisis.

All tenants are referred from the town hall, and then apply through the social security system for financial aid. For such a basically furnished house, with a through dining room-lounge, well equipped kitchen, together with the bedrooms and bathroom, they pay £64 per week rent and rates. This is a much more viable proposition for the local council than the cost of a hotel room on a bed-and-breakfast basis.

Clacton is something of a pioneer scheme, and several other councils are showing a good deal of interest. The town council is helping with management costs during the first three years of the scheme. Plans are now well afoot for a total of forty flats on the same site, for single homeless people. Some of these individuals presently have to be accommodated, albeit briefly, in one of the houses, which precludes the more valid use of those premises for families.

The important part of the scheme is the regular daily contact, helpful advice and counsel which Mrs Wright can offer. The tenants who come, sometimes for quite a number of months before the council can rehouse them, are often confused and emotionally upset. They need the supportive understanding and concern which Jean is there to provide. She told me that she has learned a great deal about housing, social security and other aspects of the problems confronting the tenants. She has established good relationships with the various local authority and government offices in the town.

The chief reasons for homelessness have already been mentioned: mortgage repayment default, due to unexpected illness, redundancy or failure of a business; abandonment of a young woman, pregnant or with a child, by a live-in partner; as well as the occasional disaster such as fire destroying the home. Jean recounted one or two stories of people who had passed through this complex and eventually re-established themselves in dignity, following humiliation by a deserting spouse. Whatever the rights and wrongs of such situations, and however foolishly or fecklessly some people may act, there is a need for someone to come alongside them and help them through the crisis. The aim is to set them on the way back to a more normal, stable pattern of life. Jean and Tom are such people. Says Tom, 'I don't think of them as problem people, rather as people with a problem.' And behind this couple is the expertise and Christian motivation of the SAHA staff, who see their role as providing a home for those who are without one, however temporarily.

The many difficulties of homelessness cannot be resolved quickly. That is true of other forms of social and moral blight in our present-day society; such as unemployment, the breakdown of family life, and poverty. Even if the necessary number of dwellings could somehow be produced by waving a magic wand, there would still be homeless people.

Amid the continuing debate as to how best to ease the housing shortage, the Salvation Army sees a vital Christian role for itself within its wide-ranging caring programmes. Providing a home for the homeless must be at least as valid as securing 'clothing for the naked' or 'food for the hungry and thirsty'. Teaching these people how to create a home for themselves is surely even more important than simply 'taking them in as strangers' (see Matthew 25:34–40). Helping people to discover (sometimes rediscover) their true worth and dignity as human beings is a vital step in creating the hope which is contained in the gospel. The good news is that there is hope for those in despair; hope in Jesus Christ. That hope may sometimes arise out of tribulation, when accepted in perseverance so as to produce character. It is then that the individual can find genuine hope (see Romans 5:3–4). The Salvationist approach to all the problems outlined so far in this volume is marked by Jesus' teaching about God, who loves each one personally. If Christ died for the outcast, the lost and sinful, then Christians must be willing to live for them as neighbours who are to be loved 'as ourselves'.

7
Home—and Dry?

Throughout history people have resorted to the use of alcohol or other drugs to achieve certain moods. In some instances they aimed to create at least some oblivion, particularly if their lives were harsh. For others, the resultant state of euphoria meant temporary liberation from taboos and conventions. This sometimes led to anti-social behaviour, often involving wild forms of promiscuous sexual activity. The name of Bacchus (or Dionysius), the Greek god of wine, has given us the word 'bacchanalian' to describe such behaviour.

Various physical and psychological consequences of such indulgence were identified centuries ago. The social disruption, including acts of crime, caused while 'under the influence'—have been experienced by one generation after another. Yet we humans are slow to learn. The degree of social acceptability of such conduct has varied, often in conjunction with swings in general standards of morality within a culture.

We only have room here simply to emphasise the growing alarm felt in society about abuse leading to addictive dependence. There is increasing public awareness of the effects of drink upon drivers and other road users. Alcohol and other drugs are perceived as the origin of much violent crime. The effects of alcohol are often at the root of marital discord and family break-up. A great deal of absenteeism from places of employment can be traced back to unwise, even disastrous over-consumption.

None of this is new, as a brief reading of social history shows. As far as this book is concerned, we cannot do better than go back to the observations of William Booth. *In Darkest England* contains some extremely pertinent comments on the subject. Drunkenness is referred to repeatedly as one of the major causes of poverty, depravity, squalor and general misery. It would be dishonest to say that the situation has changed during the intervening hundred years.

Men spent their wages on drink, leaving their families destitute. They still do in some parts of the country. Drunken men and women committed acts of folly and violence which they would not have dreamed of doing while sober. In a chapter on homelessness Booth wrote of darkest England as 'consisting broadly of three concentric circles'. They were inhabited respectively by 'the starving and home- less, but honest poor', 'those who live by vice' and 'those who exist by crime'. He then commented that all three of these circles were 'sodden with drink'.

Later, this keen observer of the way of life of the poorer segment of society in Victorian London wrote of drunken- ness as one of the vices which 'remains so little disguised, even from those who practise [it]'. He described, from direct experience, the difficulty of dealing with drunkards as 'almost insurmountable'. The effects of strong drink were passed on from one generation to another, to the extent that many children were 'not so much born into this world, but damned into it' (a quotation from a fellow-Christian reformer). Said Booth,

> There are thousands [of boys] who were begotten when both parents were besotted with drink, whose mothers saturated themselves with alcohol every day of their pregnancy, who may be said to have sucked in a taste for strong drink with their mothers' milk, and who were surrounded from childhood with opportunities and incitements to drink.

He referred subsequently to such men as 'poor wretches, born slaves of the bottle, predestined to drunkenness from their mother's womb'.

Quoting statistics for numbers of public houses in Britain (190,000 at the time), and for arrests due to drunkenness (200,000 annually), he gave his opinion that 'nine-tenths of our poverty, squalor, vice and crime spring from this poisonous tap-root'. He reminded his readers that 'the temptation to drink is strongest when want is sharpest and misery most acute'.

There are still areas of deprivation in Britain, particularly in inner-urban districts, where much the same pattern is reported by Salvationists and others working among the poorer communities. At the other end of the economic spectrum, we have extremely highly paid younger men, working principally in the speculative financial institutions in the City, behaving in a thoroughly disgusting manner at a nearby railway station on their way home from the office on a Friday evening. We have the now familiar phenomenon of lager louts who, under the influence of too much alcohol, cause mayhem every weekend. Often the brawls and vicious attacks upon rival gangs, police and even members of the public take place in normally peaceful and law-abiding villages and small country towns. Added to this are the regular media reports of the effects of alcohol upon a significant minority of football supporters.

Linked to alcohol abuse is the more recent advent of addictive drugs on a massive scale. People of all ages and every social stratum consume one or more of the narcotics: for example heroin, cocaine and its latest derivative, crack. Despite strenuous efforts by customs officers and other law enforcement personnel, illegal shipments of such highly expensive poisons continue to enter the country.

A wide range of medical, welfare and similar agencies are endeavouring to warn youngsters, in particular, of the enormous risks involved. Schools are trying to bring home the stark realities of drug abuse to children of even pre-teenage years. As an alternative to the shock tactics of showing the brutal facts of drug abuse, a serious effort is now being made by educational authorities to encourage the kind of lifestyle which does not need to resort to such practices. Yet many children and adolescents are still being accosted by drug-peddlars near school gates, in youth clubs and disco halls. It is happening under the very noses of respectable citizens who are often unaware of the significance of a little cluster of young people, apparently discussing some harmless matter.

The situation at present seems to be almost uncontainable. Police forces across the country are gravely concerned, in anticipation of a worsening of the position. The horrors of the USA scene are repeatedly presented to the general public by the news media; yet the lemming-like race towards destruction continues, apparently unabated. There seems to be no present solution to this vast and growing problem.

Advances in medical and psychological research have helped to identify and clarify the consequences of alcohol abuse in particular. A distinction is made between drunkenness and alcoholism. The latter has been defined by some as an illness caused by over-consumption, which produces dependence—or addiction. Most authorities consider alcoholism as more of a social, psychological and spiritual problem than medical. The World Health Organisation does not include it in its list of diseases.

It is nevertheless possible for some alcoholics, if they have sufficient will-power and determination, to be rehabilitated. Men and women are able to 'kick the habit'. That represents a certain 'medical' success, (cure would be an over-statement; it is much more a question of conversion).

Where alcohol is readily available, people will use it. Today supermarkets and a very wide network of licensed premises provide an alternative to the pub as a source of supply. Also, the price can be very determinative. Few would accept that alcohol is cheap here. Yet, given the appalling consequences of excessive drinking, it is hard to understand why the present government has not raised the duty on alcohol—at least in line with rising inflation. Experience in many countries has shown that price increases lead to reduced consumption. This in turn leads to a diminishing of the number of accidents, illnesses and crime.

Strong representations have been made to the ministerial group on alcohol misuse, proposing health hazard warnings on bottles or other containers, as with cigarettes. These have not been accepted. Yet the Army receives financial aid from government sources to help support its rehabilitation centres for alcoholics! This is an ambulance at the foot of the cliff rather than a fence at the top. A corpse or severely damaged person at the bottom, where there might have been a survivor at the top.

The truth is that alcohol consumption is still more socially acceptable in Britain than in a number of other western, industrialised nations. And this despite the well-publicised risks. Ninety per cent of our population take alcohol in one form or another, at least occasionally. The majority drink responsibly. A significant minority, however, are costing the whole nation very dearly.

Alcohol is not always bad for one's health, in contrast to tobacco. Some people would say that drinking is sociable, and can be fun. The same people will nevertheless usually acknowledge the cost of alcohol abuse, in human terms as well as financial. Up to 1,000,000 people in Britain suffer serious health damage through alcohol misuse. Almost 200,000 hospital admissions a year are related to alcohol. Damage to the liver, heart, kidneys and brain are some of the physical dangers of excessive drinking. The psychological and emotional harm is even greater.

More than 10,000,000 working days a year are lost in industry and commerce due to over-consumption of alcohol. One in five accidents at work involves an excessive intake.

Many thousands of senior executives use alcohol to combat stress in their work, thereby often creating an even greater problem for themselves. Nationally it is estimated that £43m is spent every day on buying drink—£30,000 a minute—and the annual health costs of abuse are around £2bn.[1]

The number of fatal accidents caused by drivers with more than the legal limit of alcohol in the blood is reported to have declined over the past ten years. If that can be substantiated it is good news, though relative: there are still 1,500 deaths on the road each year directly attributable to drinking and driving. The government has not yet reacted to considerable pressure from a number of sources—including the Army's representation—for the legal limit to be reduced to 50mg per 100ml. The present permitted level is 80mg, which many medical and other authorities hold to be too high for safety. And the list goes on: mental illness, suicide, crime and accidents of every kind.

The problem begins early. Many young people drink regularly and, all too often, heavily while still at school. Delegates to a conference of school masters and mistresses in the spring of 1989 blamed media advertising. Their criticism was that the publicity 'makes drinking seem smart, sophisticated, up-market and adult'. There is a clear case for tightening controls on alcohol promotion. Perhaps it should be permitted only at the point of sale.

So long as alcohol is associated in people's minds with social standing, manliness, even elegance, tragic consequences will continue. While advertising goes on pumping out the desirability of tasting the delights of this or that form of alcohol, the 'social debris' will continue to accumulate in hospitals, psychiatric clinics, prisons and every kind of emergency shelter.

Reverting for a moment to William Beveridge's commentary on Booth's scheme of reclamation and reform, it is interesting that he nowhere refers to the drink problem. His remarks, quoted in some detail in an earlier chapter, cover the main subjects of Booth's concerns: unemployment, poverty, exploitation, poor housing and so on—but not alcohol. Perhaps Beveridge never had to deal with any of the hundreds of thousands brought down in life by alcohol abuse. Or he may simply have felt that 'the drunk you have always with you'. There are still many people today, in high and influential positions in society and government, who would prefer to ignore the realities of the subject.

It would be quite unrealistic to expect the whole nation to 'go dry'. The aftermath of the Prohibition laws in the USA has shown quite clearly that people will go on drinking, whatever the consequences. They will enjoy it, as long as it does not begin to destroy them. In any event, legislation alone cannot determine anyone's choice in such matters. There is a great need for a much keener awareness of the risks, which have been well tabulated now. With that, there must be a measure of discipline much stronger than exists at present if the tragic outcome of drinking is to be significantly diminished. This is not simply a matter of 'consenting drinkers in private'. The behavioural aberrations resulting from excessive drinking inevitably affect other people very directly, as we have noted.

Because he saw the potential for evil inherent in alcohol consumption, Booth insisted that those who became soldiers (full members) of the Salvation Army should totally abstain from its use in any form. That remains a cardinal condition for Salvationists today. One has only to see the extent of the problem as represented in the dozens of Army centres here, not to mention hundreds of such places around the world today, which receive victims of drink, to understand this principle. The influence of such an example is very powerful. It demonstrates the possibility of an alcohol-free lifestyle which is nevertheless rich and rewarding.

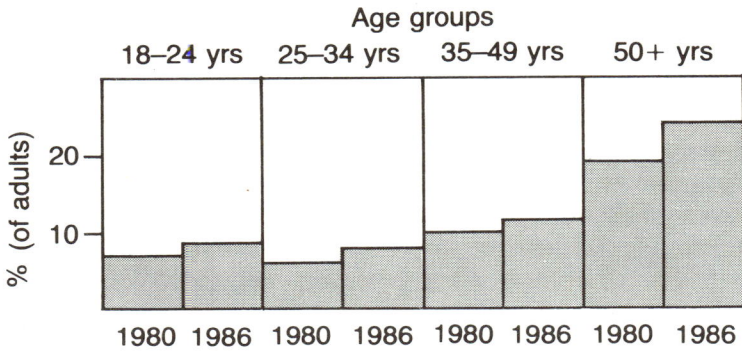

UK — Trends in non-drinking (alcohol) by age groups.

Meanwhile, someone needs to be available for the almost impossible task of rescuing and rehabilitating those who seriously want to overcome their drink problem. We have already seen in the previous chapters that there is a nation-wide network of Salvation Army work directed at such people. We have observed that almost all the forty hostels house a considerable number of victims of drink. There has been mention of rehabilitation centres, and at least one officer has been referred to as engaged in such a programme, who himself came from such a situation. He is not the only one, either, as we shall see.

It will perhaps be helpful to repeat here that Salvation Army work is often undertaken in co-operation with other associations. Even where this is not the case, the experience and research of others proves very valuable. A good deal of research is currently in progress into the origins and nature of addiction. Why do people choose to use any form of drug, including alcohol and tobacco? The creation of a new national research centre on this subject was announced in the summer of 1989. The problem is described as 'massive and growing'.

Addiction is not confined to consumables. 'Workaholism' is a well-known phenomenon. Gambling, including addiction to pin-machines, is a serious problem for some. Army personnel dealing with those who have developed a dependence upon one or more of these addictive things look for indications of any emotional problem which underlies the addiction.

The Salvation Army has urged the government to use the collective experience and understanding of alcoholism in its deliberations. General Eva Burrows, the present international leader of the Army, has herself held senior responsibility within the movement's social operations in Britain. In her present capacity she entered into formal correspondence with the Prime Minister on the subject of alcohol abuse. Mrs Thatcher replied, assuring the General that various measures were being taken to curb the incidence of this social blight. She specifically mentioned the establishment of a ministerial group to deal with the misuse of alcohol.

General Burrows wrote again, expressing appreciation for what the Prime Minister had said. However, as the Army press reported at the time (autumn 1988), the General urged Mrs Thatcher to 'include representation from voluntary bodies and professional groups working in this field'. She added, 'Such grass-roots experience would add an invaluable dimension to the research.' The Army's experience shows clearly that every drinker is a potential misuser of alcohol. 'The trend will not be reversed without radical measures,' stated General Burrows, while acknowledging that 'it will take time for the country as a whole to adjust to and accept this fact'.

In conclusion, the Army's widely-experienced woman leader assured the Prime Minister of 'the Army's skilled and compassionate commitment to those whose lives have been damaged by alcohol misuse'.

Within the Army's programme for alcoholics in Britain

there are seven rehabilitation centres and three units where drying out (detoxification) can take place under controlled conditions. The latter are quite small. The one in London (Whitechapel) has the capacity for eleven men, and the other two—in Greenock and Southampton—are able to take up to five men at a time. Davis House, in Swindon, has emergency facilities for half a dozen, as and when other local centres dealing with such people may be full.

The programme varies. At Fewster House, Greenock, the detoxification (detox for short) regime covers a seven-day period and no drugs are used. A man must truly want to undergo this often painful and depressing experience. Without that determination there can be no success. Patients must remain within the unit, in pyjamas and dressing gown. Their day time clothing is taken and kept elsewhere for them. In this clinic-like room, with simple beds and bedside lockers, the necessary isolation can be achieved. Trained staff are on hand to help, encourage when necessary and to ensure that the conditions are fulfilled. The basis of the programme is that total withdrawal from alcohol enables the body to adjust to doing without it. This does not cure the patient; at best, it is the beginning of a long and far from easy process of stabilisation and rehabilitation.

In contrast, the process at the Mountbatten Centre in Southampton is shorter, and drugs may be used on a diminishing basis. They are supposed to reduce the desire for drink. The period is usually three to four days, though individuals react variously, as with any other kind of medical attention. In both centres a doctor is on twenty-four-hour call in case of emergency. Some of the care assistants, in Southampton at least, have themselves been through this programme. It is perhaps an open question—for a medical layman—as to which programme is preferable. Does it make the work harder, or easier, if the carer is fully aware of what the patient is passing through?

The more significant point to be made is that only men

who have drunk heavily over a long period of time come to such a unit. Most are referred from a wide variety of backgrounds, but there is the possibility of self-referral. As I waited, speaking with a member of staff in Southampton, one such man came through the front door. A glance was sufficient to convey that he had been through some pretty rough times—as he himself said, when asked how the staff could help him. As the young Salvationist led him away for further discussion, I just hoped he would make it.

Captain and Mrs George Thompson were in charge of the work in Fewster House, Greenock, when I went there. I had heard that they received only men in their detox unit. Did they ever receive a woman, I wondered. By way of reply, Thompson referred me to Jenny, who has worked here for many years, and knows the score. Her own husband mis-used alcohol for a long time, living rough and eventually losing both legs. But he has finally been converted, and is now employed within the centre. So Jenny (Mrs Janet Small) has seen the problem from two sides. In fact, she has since been appointed as officer in charge here.

She emphasised that a woman is much more complex emotionally. Hence the drying-out process is that much more difficult for her. Also, women tend to cover up an alcohol problem much more effectively than men. In passing, I reflected on a fact revealed by my various visits: women do better than men in many types of breakdown or emergency—homelessness, marriage failure or financial crisis. They are nevertheless more vulnerable to alcohol damage than men. A woman's body has more fat and less water than a man's. Thus the alcohol is more concentrated in her system, and her body can more easily be harmed than a man's.

That is not to say that women do not over-indulge in strong drink. Nor are victims of alcoholism only from working-class backgrounds. Thompson related the story of the wife of a senior military officer serving abroad. She began attending such social functions as cheese and wine parties, to relieve the boredom of her life. She began to drink more and more until she was forced to admit that she was addicted. Her husband finally divorced her, leaving her in this country when he returned overseas. She began to wander, living rough despite a cultured up-bringing. She finally found her way to the Salvation Army centre, where help was available.

Standing at the window of the Thompsons' modest apartment on the premises, I gazed over the wide sweep of the River Clyde. How often we had anchored just there during World War Two! How busy the 'dockyard maties' had always been in those days in the extensive ship-building and repair yards which so dominated the area. Today all trace of those former work places for thousands of men has disappeared. They looked decidedly derelict when I last visited Strathclyde three years earlier.

What does that mean in terms of unemployment and social upheaval, I wondered. 'What can you do for a man who completes the rehabilitation programme for alcoholics?', I asked. 'Can he find a job round here?' The reply was hesitant. Unemployment has been rife here, and the situation is by no means fully resolved yet. However, new factories and other types of work have come in. IBM have a very large centre just along the coast. It is still difficult, though every effort is made to help those looking for work once they have become stabilised.

The total population of Fewster House, named after a highly respected former leader of Salvation Army Social Services in Britain, is sixty-six. Just one-third of those places are reserved for those with alcohol-related problems. The programme, which is flexible in length, may last several months if necessary. An important part of this consists of group therapy. Individual problems are aired and shared by those comprising a group, and a measure of healing begins. It always helps to know that one is not alone in any particular difficulty. There has to be frankness and openness with oneself and with others in the group.

Facilities exist for work therapy. Advice and instruction are given in a variety of practical aspects of personal life. Social and recreational activities are organised. The men are also required to keep their own areas clean. In all, the course is designed to create greater self-understanding and aware-ness, and to prepare participants for independent living. All possible help is given in such important matters as housing and employment. The management of the centre and the relevant offices of the regional authority co-operate with a view to the resettlement of each man, in time.

It is more than 400 miles from Greenock to Southampton. Yet much the same work is undertaken by the staff of the Army's Mountbatten Centre there. The spirit and motiva-tion are the same. The physical surroundings and some details of the programme vary; that is quite natural. Each officer in charge will have his own ideas as to the best way of helping those who so desperately need it. Here in Southampton the programme is more extensive, partly because a higher percentage of the men are alcoholics. Only fifteen of the sixty-five residents are here for other reasons. Ten of these are men designated as 'frail elderly', and five places are reserved for women. Some of these are in need with alcohol problems. Thus there are at least fifty places for victims of alcoholism. There is also the detoxification unit already referred to.

Mountbatten Centre is a solid-looking, late nineteenth-century building, formerly used as a seamen's home. It was known as Oxford House until renamed in 1981 in honour of Earl Mountbatten, following his death in 1979. The officers in charge at the time of my visit were Captain and Mrs Terence Pattison. He is another of those who are able to minister all the more effectively to men with this problem, because of his own years of fighting the habit. On arrival at the centre's reception office, I first met John. He had the 'pukka' accent which betrays an ex-Indian Army officer. He told me he had been a tea-planter out there too. But always—the drink. He landed back in Britain, and first came to the Mountbatten Centre some years ago. He went through the programme, but relapsed. (It is not unusual for a man to do that, possibly several times. One man, found dead on a local park bench, had been to the centre ten times, but each time took himself off again.)

'But it was no good,' said John. 'No good at all!' He might have been speaking of some useless sepoy in India, to judge by his voice. In fact, he spoke movingly of his own long battle with drink. He was now stabilised, to the point of being the trusted receptionist at this place. I would love to see the face of any Cockney vagrant alcoholic on being addressed in such tones at the office window! Yet John is another of the many miracles of divine grace, liberated from a real form of slavery, and kept straight (and dry) day by day.

Ted works in the same office. He is a qualified accountant and is now the social work administrator of this extensive programme. Pattison spoke highly of him. Yet a few years ago, he too came here and went through the programme. Another man rehabilitated and freed to fulfil his considerable potential.

Such men do not usually become Salvationists, though a few may. They do not all claim membership of any particular Christian denomination. They do recognise that it is through the power of God, in Jesus Christ, that they have become 'a new creation' in him (2 Cor 5:17).

The theme of this whole programme is 'A new life'. The motif, seen on their printed matter, their vehicles and elsewhere around the premises—and indeed, around the city—depicts this clearly. A sawn-off tree stump, bare and apparently lifeless, but with just a single sprig shooting from it, new leaves unfolding.

In many respects the programme of rehabilitation and the

follow-up towards resettlement and reintegration in society, is much the same as in other centres. Any with mental problems are assessed in a local psychiatric unit. These people come from many and varied situations but, as Pattison put it, 'All come from failure.'

The work therapy programme here is quite fascinating. Foremost among the various crafts in which the men can employ their skills is picture-framing. There is also wood-work of various kinds, weaving (they must have made their own loom) and printing. But pictures need frames—so frames are made. An account of this particular aspect of the programme appeared in *Mitre*, a trade magazine for all kinds of framing. The article was simply entitled—very appropri-ately—'Framing as a Salvation'.

The work is done on the premises, where there are quite well-equipped workshops. The sales outlet is situated just across the road. The combined operation is called 'Mayflower Craft'. (The symbolism of this name is clear. The Pilgrim Fathers set out in the 'Mayflower' in 1620, to establish a new life for themselves in the New World.) The shop is quite new and very smartly furbished. It is rented from the proprietors of the office block in which it is situated. Hundreds of pictures are on view here, all for sale. Framed tapestry work, small stools with woven seats and a few small artistic articles (duck egg shells made into trinkets and beautifully lacquered—donated for sale) are also on display.

Some shipping companies provide pictures of their own vessels for framing. They are then used in their offices, on their ships or for general publicity. Firms value the quality of the work done by the men at Mountbatten. Local artists have their works framed, and the shop serves as a sales outlet. The proceeds are shared between each artist and the centre. Tony James, the shop manager, was enthusiastic: 'There's a real purpose behind all this!'

The surplus on this trade goes entirely to help fund the

rehabilitation work. Further income is derived from another initiative, based on a very widespread Salvation Army programme in the USA. A number of containers for used clothing are placed at strategic sites in the surrounding area, as well as in the city itself, thanks to the co-operation of local authorities. People with surplus clothing to donate simply leave the garments in these, and one or two trucks circulate daily to empty them. The articles are returned to premises used by the centre. The saleable clothing is then dry-cleaned and displayed for sale. The rest is sorted as to type of textile and sold in bulk.

This operation brings in additional financial resources for the work—a very useful form of self-support. Much more significantly, the work is carried out mainly by some of the men being helped. They feel useful again. They are in employment. What they produce in this way is an important part of the therapy which will hopefully enable them eventually to resume their places in society.

There is also the 'New Life' charity shop just next to the centre. Supervised by local Salvationist volunteers and other Christian friends, this serves several purposes. Useful items are available at very reasonable prices, as with any such charitable enterprise. It is also a drop-in centre, where people can come for a social chat—which often turns out to be a spiritual conversation. Friendships are formed, and for a few the contact has been an introduction to one of the Salvation Army corps in the area. Salvationists from those congregations can also make contact with the excellent work being carried on at the centre. Finally—and by no means insignificantly—a further very useful source of income is created for the redemptive work which goes on twenty-four hours a day, seven days a week, just next door. Many a person, destitute and hopeless, has received new life there.

On the subject of converted alcoholics, Captain Richard Cook of Davis House, Swindon, introduced me to a married couple and their son, who work there. Their stories, which have become one, are worth relating.

Barbara had gone downhill steadily, due to drink addiction. Her marriage had failed. Life as a drunken vagrant is always degrading, but it seems even more so in a woman. Eventually, however, she came to Davis House and received all possible counsel and supportive care. She improved remarkably, and finally accepted Christ as her personal Saviour.

Her son, John, had to some extent followed in his mother's footsteps—as often happens. Like her, he became addicted to drink and gambling. He realised that his life was in a mess. Seeing the transformation in her life, he decided at last to give it a try. He too has been converted. Mother and son have remained dry for more than a year now.

There is yet another strand to this family saga. Geoff had also become an alcoholic and been helped through to sobriety and stability at Davis House. Romance is no respecter of age, as is the case with Barbara and Geoff. United in marriage, they both work in the centre. Barbara has been entrusted with the responsibilities involved in the reception office of this complex of compassion and care.

Then the tail-piece. John married Pauline, a Salvationist, who is in charge of the work therapy programme there. Furry toys are made, pictures framed, a variety of forms of printing undertaken, and woodwork practised. What is Pauline's aim in this work? I didn't ask her outright, but my guess is that she would hope to see many others share the miracle of grace which has been the experience of the family into which she has married.

The Wiltshire village of Highworth is about eight miles from Davis House. Gloucester House, in the centre of the community there, is a stone building typical of the village. An unpretentious façade fails to give the passer-by any idea of the difficulties experienced behind it by those who come to this Salvation Army alcoholism rehabilitation centre.

They have come in the hope of breaking the habit. They are seeking the strength to overcome their struggles. Their average age is a good deal lower than it was just a few years ago. Many have lost their self-esteem, and some are no longer capable of making even a simple decision. They need help.

Acquired by the Army in 1961, the premises are sand-wiched between a bank and a pub, with an attractive-looking country inn immediately opposite. The lane at the rear of the building is Brewery Street. In such surroundings, the policy of helping alcoholics to stand on their own feet and resist the temptation to drink must be tested just about as strongly as it could be!

Captain and Mrs Joseph Smith carry the responsibility for the programme here. They have a professionally competent staff who are all Christians. The staff to residents ratio is just about one-to-one; this is intensive therapy. Smith spent quite some time trying to help me understand the background to such work. It was the first place I had visited with time to stop and learn.

Nine men at a time can be accommodated in this centre, and the programme is basically similar to that in the centres already described. There is close liaison with the community alcohol team and the alcoholism team operated by the district health authority. Several other inter-agency groups are also involved.

Smith spoke quietly but intensely of the deep guilt feelings experienced by many of those who go through the pro-gramme. They have failed: loved ones, friends, society and, above all, themselves. There are often profound feelings of anger and frustration. They need guidance in becoming aware of the nature and causes of their inner conflicts, and ways in which these can be resolved. Several of the officers I met, engaged in work with alcoholics, have spoken of the similarities between such counselling and that for bereaved persons. These men have to learn to accept the reality of their loss—in this case, the drink. They must discover how to adjust to that loss, and to reinvest their emotions in a new life.

On another occasion I encountered the same process being worked through in London's dockland area. At Grieg House, literally in the shadow of the overhead light railway, Captain and Mrs Nigel Collins, with their team, were attempting the same nearly impossible task. They have now taken over the direction of affairs at the Mountbatten Centre, and others equally experienced in this type of work have assumed the responsibility here in the East End of the capital.

Like their colleagues in the different centres referred to, they are proving the power of God to redeem men and women, despite the inevitable breakdowns, disappointments and failures. As long as a person wants to make good, and sincerely strives to become free from the fetters of addiction, people like the Collins, the Smiths, the Cooks and others will offer them all the resources at their disposal. If these people can eventually be resettled—preferably at home, and dry—the Army's front-line people in this on-going battle will feel that it has all been worth the very considerable effort. They are in a very real sense, as the apostle Paul said, 'shining like lights in a dark world' (Phil 2:15, Phillips).

Note

1. These statistics were obtained from literature prepared by Alcohol Concern, a London-based registered charity which specialises in research and dissemination of information on this subject.

8

Silver Threads among the Gold

To grow old is a part of the natural course of life. To grow old gracefully and happily is a less universal experience. Many find difficulties at this stage, often through declining physical and mental powers. The cycle of nature, from germination through growth, flowering and ripening, should result in the maturity of fruitfulness. Ageing should enrich life, bringing to maturity what the years of experience have produced.

Not everyone survives to old age, of course. The toll of accidents and stress-related diseases may well equal what used to be the loss through slaughter in wars. Among those who may achieve the biblical norm of 'three score years and ten' are a number who age prematurely. This can cause great distress, particularly if it is associated with some form of mental disorder such as Alzheimer's disease, or physical conditions such as rheumatism or arthritis. The sense of richness and satisfaction in maturity are often diminished as these people grow older.

Victims and their relatives, or other carers, may suffer great anguish. We use expressions such as 'a martyr to' some form of disability, to indicate the degree of pain involved, physically, mentally and emotionally.

Nevertheless, people in this country are living longer than in the past. Average life expectancy has increased considerably in a few decades. Improved health care and hygiene, together with a better understanding of nutrition, have contributed considerably to this trend. Enhanced education and a general raising of the standards of intellectual awareness of life must also be deemed as factors. By and large, people in Britain remain healthy for longer, and have more ways than ever before of enjoying even the later years of their lives.

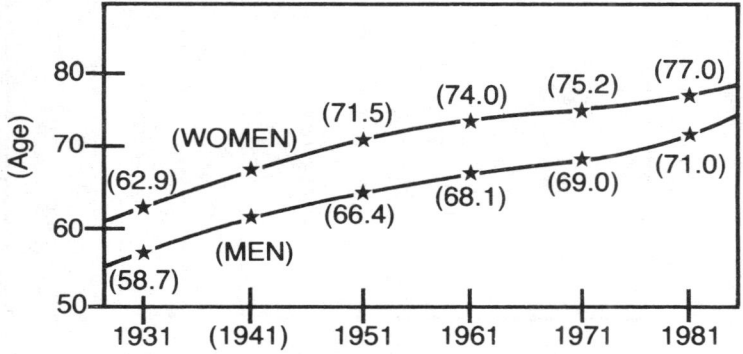

Life expectancy at birth

	1985/6	*2024/5*
Men	72.0 years	75.2 years
Women	77.7 years	80.3 years

Life expectancy at birth based on mortality rates

Several recent surveys have suggested that older people are, on the whole, having the time of their lives. A vast range of special travel and general cultural facilities are available to the over-sixties—and well beyond. It is no longer cause for special comment if a septuagenarian gains a university degree through studies, or an octogenarian travels intercontinentally. The number of clubs, societies and associations which cater for older people seems constantly to be growing. Most people do not feel themselves to be old until well into their seventies or more—and most smile and joke about being referred to as 'OAPs'.

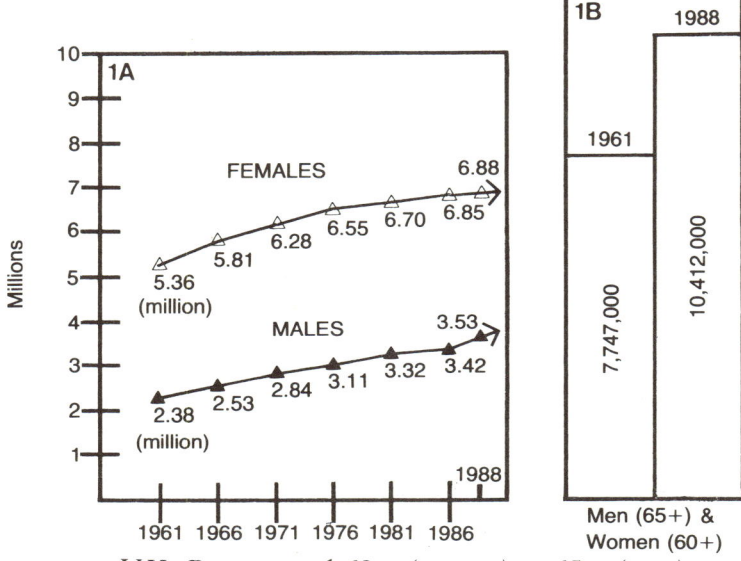

Figure 1A *UK Persons aged 60+ (women) or 65+ (men)*
Figure 1 *UK Total population: men 65+ and women 60+*

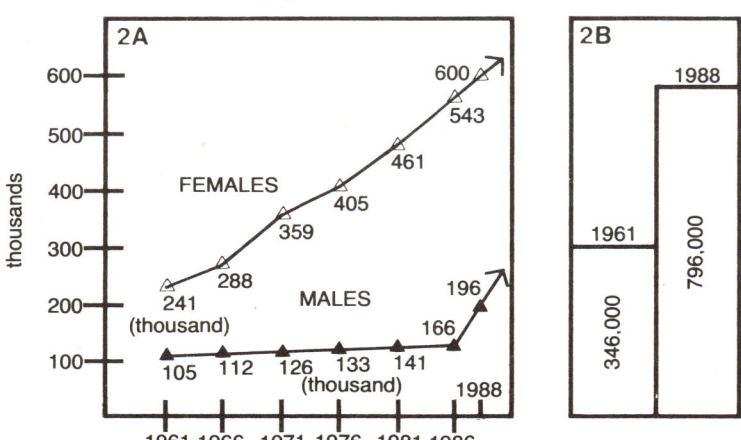

Figure 2A *UK Persons aged 85 and over*
Figure 2B *UK Totals (men and women)*

The idea of being thrown on the scrap-heap at pensionable age is much less acute than it might have been some years ago. Businesses and enterprises are actually advertising for and recruiting older people. They really need them as the number of school-leavers declines, especially in the many areas where there is a labour shortage. Provided they are physically fit, people of mature years are likely to prove more reliable than youngsters just emerging into the real world from the classroom. With smaller families, once the children have grown up and left home, there are often many years of fulfilment in work and leisure before the onset of true old age.

Yet there is a negative side to the changing patterns of society. As the number of older people increases, there will inevitably be more who need special care. As people live longer, there are bound to be more physical or mental problems. Some who suffer severe disabilities tend to become irritable, complaining about those around them and appearing to be ungrateful for what is being done for them. At a certain point those who care for them begin to think of them as being impossible. Loving concern can turn sour, and compassion can slowly wither. Only the most devoted and dedicated of carers do not succumb to these influences.

This situation seems more frequent nowadays. Relationships may even deteriorate to a point where violence is used. At first this may be quite an involuntary reaction to the circumstances; a subconscious expression of deep tensions. It is claimed that up to half a million elderly persons in this country are in danger of physical or mental abuse. The British Geriatrics Society reports that 'most carers are naturally compassionate people; it is the constant pressure on them that may make frustration and anger overspill into violence'.

Some nurses, care assistants and even relatives tend to regard the frail and feeble elderly as children, and to treat them accordingly. Recognition of their human dignity is overlooked, as is the fact that they have been young, active and useful in their time. The immediate situation seems to determine the attitude of these carers. The intense embarrassment of those who become incontinent, and thus need attention of an unpleasant nature, is seemingly ignored. For women who reach this stage, the devastating effects upon their sensitivities must be even greater than for men.

Similar comments can be made about the mentally handicapped. For those whose observable behaviour does not reflect their true nature and worth as human beings, special sensitivity and sympathy are of particular importance. It is a denial of the love of God for one person to treat another with disrespect and even contempt when they are unable to fend for themselves.

All this can happen within a family circle where the ties of kinship are usually strong. There is a much greater risk in nursing homes and similar institutions unless there is a sound professional discipline combined with genuine compassion in the care programme. Under any other conditions elderly people can quite quickly lose their personal dignity and identity. No longer able to do things for themselves, they begin to lose the will to live.

The report referred to above, 'Abuse of elderly people; an unnecessary and preventable problem', describes a typical family situation involving someone 'over 75, female, roleless, functionally impaired, lonely, fearful . . . and living at home with an adult child'. The document lists such features as 'physical assault, food deprivation, over-sedation, involuntary isolation or confinement' and even sexual abuse among the ways in which the stress of caring for the frail elderly may find expression.

The concept of 'tender loving care' needs to be fostered and encouraged by all possible means. The notion of such caring as a vocation more than a profession needs fresh emphasis. The carers need all the support which society can offer. There is no true substitute in caring for the weak and helpless.

Less dramatic, but none the less significant, is the condition of the growing number who find themselves living alone. The dispersal of the extended family, referred to in Chapter 3, makes this almost inevitable. Even where there are happy family relationships, the older members will not often find accommodation with their own children and their families. Some have become accustomed to living on their own, but for older widows or widowers the loss of a partner requires a great deal of adjustment. The fear of loneliness is often matched by a corresponding fear of being a burden to loved ones. The feeling of not being wanted, or being a nuisance can be very real. When added to the feeling of solitariness which living alone produces, a real shadow can be cast over the final years of life.

Even at a purely economical level, living alone poses problems. With limited income and even more limited savings, it is not easy to keep up with the rising cost of living. Certainly the level of state pensions does little to help on that particular point. The problem comes full circle when older people are too proud to apply for what they see—however mistakenly—as charity. Others simply do not know of, or understand how to apply for, supplementary benefits which are relevant to their situations. For yet others, it goes against the grain to feel that they are dependent upon others for their normal living expenses. Many would still prefer to deprive themselves of nourishment, or warmth in winter, than to apply—in terms of an earlier period—for relief 'on the parish', with the dreaded means test.

In all or any of these circumstances, frugality can all too easily become poverty—and such people need help. Folk in their seventies and eighties often accept such situations with a quiet dignity. They have learned the discipline of living within their means, and are not likely to change now. Yet in these sunset years, the quality of their lives may be diminished. And that is a shame, for these are very often the people whose toil and labour through the years have contributed to the prosperity of the nation. They deserve better.

The dread of being put into the workhouse, which hung over succeeding generations of older people in the nineteenth and early twentieth centuries, has gone. In his day William Booth identified these people as part of the 'submerged tenth' whom he sought to help. Attitudes have changed, policies have become more enlightened, and in practice the vast majority of elderly people will have a roof over their heads until the day they die.

Yet in place of that earlier fear has come another—more subtle but nevertheless real: the anxiety that they will have no one to look after them when they can no longer look after themselves. Where death was formerly seen by many deprived people as a merciful release, there seems to be a much greater clinging to life today. We tend to stave off the thought of dying; death is a taboo subject of conversation. Of course, for those with a strong faith and a belief in eternal life—both here and hereafter—it must be different. Yet even among believers this tendency to defer consideration of the inevitability of death is not entirely absent.

As for the concept of 'dying with dignity' (not to be confused with euthanasia), there is much to disturb the human spirit in the moral and spiritual atmosphere today. The independence which characterises many older people, sometimes to the point of being counter-productive, is not always sufficient to overcome loneliness or the fear of death. The need for a stronger spiritual faith is very great in our materialistic society. Without it, life will always be bleak for those of advancing age, together with its attendant problems.

In brief, those who are consciously approaching the end of their days on earth need a particularly firm reassurance of being loved. The faith to believe that God loves them is best conveyed in and through the compassion shown by those around them. This is ultimately the only power which can overcome the fears and confusion of age. It is the only true source of peace and serenity in the last stage of a human life. It is the greatest service anyone can offer to those who are on the final lap of life.

Some of the early–day Salvationist social workers, and others with a concern for very needy people, felt that the Army should include the elderly poor in its efforts. Soon after the publication of *In Darkest England and the Way Out*, an American Salvation Army journalist wrote a telling article for one of the movement's own periodicals. She graphically outlined the need to provide homes for these people. Major Susie Swift, then working in Britain, asked, 'Is there going to be no corner in the Social Scheme for such as Trotter Granny? What about our thrifty hard–working *old* people?' The lady referred to was old, poor and faced with the prospect of ending her days in the workhouse. Under the terms of the Poor Laws, those of advanced years, living in penury, had to appear before the local Board of Guardians. The only option open to these committees was committal to an asylum known as a workhouse.

The Salvation Army began providing accommodation for elderly people as early as 1901, in Australia. More homes were subsequently established there and in New Zealand, as well as in Norway. Only in 1910 was the first such institution opened in the United Kingdom. Whereas the principal aim in the newer countries was to combat loneliness among the aged, in Britain it was the response to poverty that prevailed in the planning.

The system of paying state pensions to the elderly was new and very limited. Major Fairbank records in *Booth's Boots* that in 1909 only those over seventy years of age were eligible, and then for just five shillings a week. Even that far from princely sum was available only to those whose other weekly income did not exceed eight shillings.

Against the background of such limited social provisions for the poorest in the population, the Army commenced what was to become a worldwide network of centres providing sheltered accommodation for elderly people who have no viable alternative once they can no longer keep home for themselves. The most recent statistics show that there are 164 Salvation Army eventide homes in a number of countries, accommodating well over 8,000 older people. Of these, thirty-nine are maintained in Britain, with places for more than 1,300 men and women. Included in these figures are just over 200 people living in independent or sheltered housing on the site of one or other of four of the homes.

In addition, there are many residents in the various Army hostels who are pensioners with no other place to live (see Chapter 6). A number of these require special care due to their extreme fragility. Most of them are men, though there is provision in some hostels for women.

Not all the eventide homes are in built-up urban areas. A number are set in beautiful surroundings. Several are large mansion-type houses standing in their own grounds. Some have been purchased, while others were bequeathed as legacies. These are not always the easiest premises to adapt for use by elderly people, and more recent homes have been purpose-built, in conformity with government requirements. All these homes are open to inspection at any time.

An important factor nowadays is that there should be a community within reach of the residents, to act as a stimulus. The able-bodied should be able to get out to the shops, meet other people and wherever possible participate in local activities.

Most of these homes are for both men and women, though a few cater for only one sex. Where that is the case, residents are encouraged as far as is practicable to get out and about, and to meet both men and women. Captain Alan Hart, the energetic and progressive District Officer for the Army's social homes in Ulster, related an interesting anecdote.

Among the half-dozen social centres in the province are

two eventide homes. One, just outside Belfast, is for men, and the other, in the city's outskirts, is for women. For many years there had been little or no direct contact between the residents of the two places. When it was recently suggested that this situation should be remedied, the staff were quite amused at the reactions. The men brightened up visibly, and smartened themselves even more visibly, for this unaccustomed 'confrontation', while the ladies preened themselves. Since then, I learned, this perfectly natural form of social mixing has become a regular part of the programme in both places. I have been told that romances occur in the eventide homes from time to time, though I do not know of any specific instances. But then, who needs statistics when Cupid's arrows are loosed?

The role of the Salvation Army housing associations in England, Wales and Scotland has already been mentioned (see Chapters 3 and 6). Apart from the sheltered housing complexes they own and operate independently, they have financed and constructed a number of centres for which the Salvation Army Social Services act as agents. Several of these are designed for elderly people.

The sheltered housing recently opened in St Helens, Lancashire, differs from some other such complexes in that the association has also constructed a Salvation Army corps building on the site, in conjunction with the Army's British Territory ('field') administration.

The programme of this reopened corps is quite independent of the housing units, though residents are naturally welcome if they wish to attend the meetings or share in any other activities. These include special gatherings for over-sixties and for women of any age.

Sunnyside, in Edinburgh, is typical of another kind of complex. The eventide home, as such, is in a large, modern building, with accommodation for around thirty people. Adjacent is sheltered housing consisting of thirty-six single and fourteen double units, and independent units for another twenty-eight people. A variant of this stands on a site on the edge of Tunbridge Wells. For very many years the main building has been a home for retired Salvation Army officers —Sunset Lodge. Now the housing association has constructed two sheltered housing blocks in the grounds. These combine the character and charm of the 'big house' with the functional facilities of purpose-built units for one or two people. This type of joint project has considerably increased the number of older people who can be allocated housing in retirement, and eventually full residential care, if and when necessary.

To discover some of the traditional character of an eventide home, as well as of current trends in enhanced care of those at varying stages of dependence, I visited two of the inner London centres. Alver Bank in Clapham is now a three-part housing complex. There is independent housing for up to fifty people, in twenty-five one-bedroom flats; and sheltered housing units consisting of six bed-sitting rooms and two small flats. All this accommodation is new, having been built in the extensive grounds of the main building. The latter was extensively refurbished, and reopened in 1986 as a registered home for the elderly.

A little further across South London stands Rookstone, in the Sydenham area. Purpose built in the 1960s, this building has recently been refurbished and modernised so that the staff will be able to deal adequately with an increasingly frail population. Nowadays the distinction between those needing residential care (Part III) and full nursing home facilities is becoming more difficult to define. Major Doreen Ingram, the officer in charge, and her staff colleagues, cope very devotedly with very dependent people, so that most can die with dignity in what has become their home. Only when they need specific or specialised medical aid which calls for hospital admission is this arranged.

There is clearly a much more mixed population with a greater range of mobility at Alver Bank. The independent units are just that: places where older people can live without any form of supervision. The sheltered housing is situated in the new wing of the main building, where residents have the support of a warden who makes daily contact. In both these areas of the complex occupants have their own furniture, and pay their rent through the Army's Social Services to the housing association.

Those needing residential accommodation with full care, are housed in the old building, which now has furnished single rooms rather than the former large shared rooms. Applicants for admission must be able to manage most things for themselves when they enter, though limited medical care is available as and when needed later. Every effort is made to avoid disruptive residents, for the good of the great majority. It is nevertheless inevitable that a few will at some stage need psychiatric attention. Referrals to the geriatric unit of St Thomas' Hospital, housed in the nearby South-West Hospital, are made through the local general practitioner. She makes regular fortnightly visits.

Excellent relationships have been built up between the staff of the home and local medical, social and housing personnel. There is close and constant contact with the local DSS office staff. The pensions of the eventide home residents are collected, and distributed after deducting board. This is all in conformity with the established scales, and the staff appear to have virtually no difficulty on this account.

As required under present legislation, there is a qualified and competent care staff in each of these homes. The key-worker system is in operation, by which one care worker is allocated four or five residents and remains in regular contact. Any special needs, or any change in a resident's physical or mental health, are included in the worker's responsibilities. A care co-ordinator brings together the observations and findings of the key workers, ensuring the maximum benefit to each resident.

Having described the three separate sectors of this complex, I must add a comment about the community centre situated in the grounds. In one sense it is the heart of the community, the place where independent or sheltered residents can meet with those of the home. Sometimes older people from the neighbourhood share in the various activities here, though with limited accommodation there have to be some restrictions. Those living in their own flats can come into the lounges of the main building to share companionship too. There is a remarkable integration, fostered and encouraged by the officer in charge, Major Marion Henderson and her deputy, Major Dorothy Caddy.

I visited Vi, one of the independent residents. She told me how she had been offered this place which was 'so nice and cosy', by the Lambeth Borough housing department (they have control of fifty per cent of the places). Speaking of the loneliness in a three-bedroom house in which she lived for twenty-five years after her husband died, and long after her children had left home, she pointed to one of her kitchen chairs. 'It's one I got with my coupons during the war. Do you remember?' Happily I did, and smiled as she tried to work out how many times she had given it 'a new lick of paint'. Certainly the legs, seat and back looked a good deal thicker than they probably were originally.

Vi became a little shy when I asked her what sort of community activities she enjoyed. She spoke of films, concerts and physical exercise. Suddenly she blurted out, giggling a little, 'Me and a few others 'ave started our own over-sixties choir.' That momentous secret having been divulged, she went on to describe the marvellous feeling of being in such good company, with her own independence but with someone always available to talk with when necessary. Her next-door neighbour, Mrs H, applied from the Isle of Wight, through Salvation Army sources. Her four children are 'all lovely', but they rarely managed to see her, and loneliness was a real source of pain following her husband's death. Now she has the companionship of people of her own age and of similar interests, and 'the meetings are lovely'. So says a lifelong Salvationist.

Not every resident is equally happy. One woman resident is depressive, dogmatic and domineering. Her husband has got used to this, but doesn't find her constant complaining and criticism easy. Yet she is physically handicapped and needs this kind of semi-independent living. When things get too 'hot' for him, there is always a lounge to escape to until his life-partner has cooled down a little!

Even those confined to a wheelchair are included in some form of physical exercise. Some prove very adept. Those who give guidance and instruction in this important aspect of the residents' lives are well qualified. They know the limits which need to be observed, and encourage everyone to enter into the exercise programme to the best of their ability. It is sometimes difficult for the staff to know how far to go in trying to persuade reluctant residents to join in with this. They need it, but there is a limit to the extent to which one can use pressure against a person's own will. Some residents, although physically disabled, get around the home wonderfully well. The use of walking-frames has made a considerable difference. These aids, sometimes referred to as 'zimmers', enable certain 'drivers' to 'zim' around the house with remarkable swiftness!

With careful budgeting, the costs of running such a place can just about be covered. The DSS figure (at the time of writing) is £147.50 a week per person, though where special care is involved this may rise to £173. Residents receive £9.55 for personal expenses, though the majority do not seem to need it all. Some have accumulated considerable sums in the course of time. This level of government support for people in homes is in great contrast to conditions in Victorian times, but that progress is still relative. It costs the state a good deal less to keep an elderly person in a residential home than to maintain a prisoner in a grossly over-crowded prison.

There is something very pathetic about a person whose mental powers begin to decline. To be in full possession of one's intellectual faculties into old age is a great blessing. Percy, aged ninety-eight, lives in the sheltered housing area, and still has his bass trombone in his cupboard. On special occasions (such as my visit) he gets it out, dusts it down, makes a few futile attempts to 'have a blow', before regaling people with stories of his seventy-odd years as an Army bandsman. His mind is clear; he is fortunate.

By contrast, it was impossible to have any kind of conversation with an exceptionally gifted Salvation Army officer, whose poetry and songs have been used with great blessing all around the world by Salvationists. She suffers from Alzheimer's disease. She appears to be quite happy, oblivious to what goes on around her. But sadly she can no longer recognise her own songs when spoken or sung to her. And she is not alone. Deterioration of the brain is one of several sad features of ageing. It tests the dedication of the staff, who have to try to find ways of communicating. Yet the very existence of a home like this is a great blessing for those so afflicted—and for their relatives. It is yet another of those shafts of light which brighten what would otherwise be a very sombre form of existence for those concerned.

The present programme at Rookstone is much the same as that in Alver Bank. Devoted care, stimulating activities and the spiritual support of daily prayers, Bible study and related activities, become increasingly important as people become older. Facing the ultimate truth about life and death, these people are very often greatly comforted by the reassurance of what is ultimately most important: the existence of God, his love for each of his creatures, and the knowledge that they may commune with him even in times of greatest physical frailty and mental confusion.

That is certainly one of the principal differences between simply 'a home for old people' and one of the Army's deeply caring residential centres for the elderly. These places are much more than just a few more units in a national network of government sponsored homes. They represent he who came into the world to be 'the light of men', and the influence of the Spirit of Christ is the transforming element in the lives of those who are able to spend their last years in such a place.

(For comment on non-residential programmes for older people, see Chapter 9.)

9

Into the Community

Salvationists sometimes say that the Army was born in the open air. William Booth, their founder, began his ministry by preaching as a lad in the streets of Nottingham. Later, in 1865, he accepted more extensive evangelistic responsibility in some of the public places of the East End of London. Only later did he begin to hire halls in which to hold meetings. Even then, these gatherings were designed to attract the local community, not members.

Through the years the movement's emphasis has remained on reaching out into local communities. As people were converted and subsequently decided to 'join up', there came an almost inevitable shift in this policy. The spiritual welfare of its own soldiers and other committed people assumed an importance of its own. At times this may have created a diversion from exclusive concern for others. Yet the underlying principle has remained that of going out to the people.

Bands and other groups regularly hold open-air meetings in residential streets or places where people gather. When corps officers are appointed—they are never 'called' to individual congregations—it is to the town (or other district), to command the corps there. The local community is the Army's catchment area, and Salvationists see their mission as being to evangelise among all members of that population.

The word 'community' implies a group with common interests or shared concerns. The way the word is used today, however, implies a very diverse and disparate grouping of people residing in a limited area. The communal spirit has to some extent diminished over recent decades, for several reasons. For one thing, people tend to spend their free time in their own homes, often watching television or a video. Homes are more comfortable, and there is less reason to go out, except for specific purposes. This is a vast change from the times when one walked directly from the parlour onto the pavement outside, and when granny, aunts, uncles and other relatives lived on the same street. Those communities were often rough and tough, but characterised by a remarkable sense of communal loyalty and cohesion. Today we are all much more insular—and pretend we are happier. That is open to question.

The growth of large cities, merging to form huge conurbations, has furthered the erosion of community spirit. Much greater anonymity has entered into people's social life. In trying to break down this impersonal element in cities, residents have formed an increasing number of interest groups. Some of these are cultural, involving the preservation of long-established customs, and a variety of artistic and other activities. Sports and leisure clubs, and hobby groups abound. In some areas pubs are still significant centres of social life, and discos attract crowds of young people.

In many larger cities the decline in standards of housing in older districts has led to large-scale migration to newer estates, and subsequently to peripheral towns and villages. More people live at a distance from their place of employment, and the communal ties are thereby weakened.

The growth of minority ethnic groups has established many smaller, tightly-knit communities, which have generally become exclusive in character. Long-term residents have tended to exclude the new arrivals. These, in turn, have created their own communal identity, which almost automatically keeps others away. In this way, psychological and cultural barriers are erected, which are not easily removed.

It can no longer be said that all people living in a certain district form a community in the formerly accepted sense. Smaller towns are possibly less affected by this trend, but even in rural areas there is no longer the same feeling of belonging to one another.

Local, regional and national authorities have made some efforts to reintroduce the notion of genuine communities— though not always with success. In their efforts to provide better housing, some city councils have transplanted people from areas of demolition into brand-new buildings, but without any communal facilities. These newer communities then become soulless; there is no natural heart to them. In any event, such changes, and the creation of human feelings of belonging, must involve the people themselves. All too often the planning details become political issues. The social, economic and ethnic differences within a town or city are still very considerable. By and large we are still a very class-conscious nation, reluctant to see great changes introduced.

Certain initiatives, sometimes of a defensive nature, have succeeded in bringing together people living in a limited area, in a way few other developments have. The rapidly increasing number of police-sponsored neighbourhood watch groups is a good example. When well organised, local vigilante groups may serve the same purpose, though obviously there are certain risks with such schemes.

Parent-teacher groups, or other parent-based forms of association, represent another way in which local people come to know each other better. Yet in very many districts there is no one communal centre, or focal point, which is generally recognised as such. In the more distant past the church fulfilled that function. For better or worse, that is now largely a matter of history.

Nevertheless, in the midst of this complex pattern of social change, many churches have begun visiting homes in their areas. Others, who were already doing something of the kind, have quickened the pace and intensity of their out-reach. A few have tried holding street services—though not usually with the slumber-chasing clamour of a brass band at 10 am on a Sunday!

Beyond such forays, whether systematic or sporadic, is the influence of individual Christians in the communities in which they live. A degree of separation has crept in here, in that so many members of churches—including Salvationists —live a considerable distance from their places of worship. They are no longer a natural part of the community in the immediate neighbourhood of their church—or corps. The end result is a gulf between one community and another. It is a case of 'you in your small corner, and I in mine'. Left as it is, this trend would ultimately produce a truly destructive fragmentation of society, even at local level. The concept of community would then be doomed, with disastrous social consequences.

How then are Christians to reach into the most needy communities? What is to be the attitude and response of the churches to the needs of those living in the more deprived areas of our cities? It would be quite unrealistic to suggest a mass return of the more economically favoured, house-owning Christians to the inner-urban areas. In time those run-down districts may be improved and made attractive for the better off. That is beginning to happen in a number of cities, but in most cases it will take a long time. In other places it will serve only to create two quite distinct social communities in one small district. The London docklands area is a case in point.

Church leaders have been giving this matter a great deal of attention in recent years. The report of the commission appointed by the Archbishop of Canterbury, *Faith in the City*, goes into considerable and analytical detail, and makes many practical proposals. At much the same time as this group was studying a very broad scene in Britain, the Salvation Army instituted a similar survey. This was to be based on the stark realities of work currently being undertaken by Salvation Army officers and others in the inner-city areas. The so-called goodwill centres were mentioned in Chapter 2. To them must be added the practical and down-to-earth programmes operating from corps community centres.

The report which followed this research was written by Major Jean James, formerly very much involved in the goodwill programmes throughout Britain. It was based on her own observations, and discussions with those directly responsible for such operations. With the title *No Neighbours for the City?*, this document has chapter headings which underline some of the Army's long-standing concerns: 'To feel our brother's care' and 'All things to all men', for example.

Several things are clear to the Army's leadership in Britain, notably the danger of over-extending still further the existing resources to the detriment of the wider spectrum of the movement's present programmes. Current concern with church growth principles must not be neglected. This is essential if the Army is to recover and fully exercise the vital and dynamic evangelical influence which is its only *raison d'être*.

On some matters it is important to recognise the impossibility of turning back the clock—let alone the calendar. Many Salvationists, like their counterparts in the churches, have grown away culturally from the population in which their parents and grandparents were nurtured—and in which they themselves may have begun life. They still go out 'into the highways and byways' with the gospel. To what extent they have succeeded in communicating the message is more open to question. Where their meetings have remained a focal point in a street, from which individuals have gone from door to door making personal contact with people, their chances of success will have been greater.

This is not the place to air views on the best methods of witnessing clearly and effectively to one's Christian faith nowadays. That must be done between Salvationists or other church-based groups. Yet the basic questions remain: How do we get through to people in their communities? What must be done to make them feel at ease when we visit them or invite them to our centres? How can the Christian message of salvation in and through Jesus Christ be communicated meaningfully to ordinary people, who have little if any notion of the gospel?

In the rest of this chapter I hope to show something of what I have recently learned about Salvation Army outreach and influence in the community. The situation is admittedly patchy, but a great deal of splendid work is being done. Many people, whose lives are blighted by some of the destructive forces at work in our society, are being helped and spiritually uplifted. Areas previously untouched or only marginally influenced by a Salvation Army ministry, are now being 'missionised' by recently appointed community chaplains. This is officially described as 'an initiative taken to break new ground and to establish work where it does not now exist'.

*   *   *

A useful starting point may be to enquire what happens in a Salvation Army goodwill centre. The simple first response is that it depends upon local needs. I visited four such places: two in quite different areas of London, and one each in Belfast and Liverpool. In addition, the work of the so-called corps on the vast Easterhouse estate in Glasgow, and in Liverpool's Childwall Valley, is in fact much closer to that of a goodwill centre than a structured corps with its established congregation.

Notting Hill is one of London's most mixed districts. The Portobello Road, renowned for its market and series of quaint shops and boutiques, spans the gulf between two utterly different groups of people. At the south end antique shops display items for sale at four-figure prices—a connoisseur's paradise. Just a few hundred yards along this relatively narrow thoroughfare are some of the drunken vagrants who spend their days and nights sleeping it off under the motorway fly-over—the Westway; a down-and-out's hell!

Halfway along the street is an old and very ordinary building—the local goodwill centre. No more than a quarter of a mile away are properties which are currently changing hands at between £1m and £2m. Actors, TV stars, members of parliament and wealthy people favour the area. Kensington Palace is less than a mile away. More close by, however, are narrow roads lined with run-down old houses, in which some of the capital's poorest people eke out an existence. It is to them, with all the deprivation and depravity which such districts seem to nourish, that Major Pat Charlsworth and her assistant, Captain Norma Richardson, minister. And what a ministry!

Of course, there are some ordinary poor and needy folk who come to the centre or whom the ladies visit. There are also those whose lives are characterised by violence, debauchery and a sense of hopelessness.

Prostitution is a normal part of community life around here. But it is the cheap and mean kind, decidedly downmarket. The further east, towards the Bayswater area, the higher the price. Sheila is one of the girls who comes to the Sunday club at the centre. She's nearly fourteen now. She has been sexually abused by her father for years, but now it's time for her to contribute towards the family budget (ie, the cost of father's booze), so he's 'put her out on the game'. Mum is past it now, having patrolled the pavements for years in search of clients—and income.

Father is a pimp, and his own daughter is virtually forced to hang around the pubs he frequents, and from which he controls his patch. Even her class-mates refer to her as a 'slag'. Is there any hope? What has her life been for as long as she can remember? Nothing but sordid drudgery. At least she finds some brightness, some sense of decency at the centre. They don't jibe at her there, nor condemn her. From the two officers she has learned something of real love. Perhaps some seed of aspiration towards a better kind of life will germinate in her one of these days. She'd like it to happen, but she's been almost damned by her environment since she was born.

Sheila is not alone in all this. Several of the local girls, who quite regularly attend the centre for the 'homeless meals', have drifted into the oldest profession in the world. No ambitions beyond making a bit more than they hand over to the pimps. No sense of regret or shame any more—or so it seems, but maybe there's still a spark of dignity somewhere within them.

Life is tough in their families. Their parents need money for drink—and some food. Is there any chance of such young women becoming adults who will fulfil their potential as citizens? Certainly Charlesworth and Richardson are not going to stop trying to help the likes of these.

Drug trafficking has gone underground to some extent in this area, mainly because of increased police vigilance. However, substances are still passed from hand to hand, as a few youngsters cluster closely to conceal the true nature of their transactions—even on the door-step of the centre. As for drink—well, William Booth would have little reason to change his assessment of alcohol abuse upon thousands of Londoners today as in his day.

Drunken brawls in the streets and assaults upon women and children in their homes are common events. For those who cannot control their craving, there is a gradual but perceptible drink-sodden descent into a state of near-total apathy. The goodwill officers respond quickly and coolly to appeals for help when drunken violence disturbs the neighbourhood. One may take a seriously injured person to the casualty ward, while the other goes to sit with the bewildered children of those involved, wide-eyed with apprehension and fear.

It would be false to imply that such happenings fill the whole week's programme, though they do occur all too often. There is much that is positive. A pensioners' luncheon club brings together some sixty people twice a week for a good basic three-course meal, for fifty pence. This is followed by a meeting, either of the local over-sixties club or of the Home League. The latter affords an excellent opportunity for the women officers to help the ladies in their efforts to create decent homes—efforts which are sometimes thwarted by events like those described above.

Home visits are made regularly where there are known, special needs. Sick folk are visited in hospital. Filthy homes are cleaned out, quite often in collaboration with local authority social workers and 'clean-up squads'. Elderly folk may need nothing more than help in completing official forms, usually in applying for supplementary benefits.

Sunday begins with a prayer meeting, involving the handful of local Salvationists and the new Christians—those just beginning in the faith. Quite a number of real conversions take place, and every possible form of prayer support and practical support is given to them. Then follows a bright meeting. There is a special get-together for the children: the Sunday club. About forty attend regularly. They like to come because they are 'loved—but not coddled'. One girl said, quite spontaneously, 'We like coming because we can talk to you, and you understand—*everything*.' From what I heard during my visit, there's not much that goes on in that district which these two neatly-uniformed, highly practical women don't know.

The area around the centre is 'darkest England' every bit as much as the East End of London was in Booth's day. And this centre is certainly a beacon of light beaming rays of hope and cheer to many.

Much more could be written, and a good deal of it would apply equally to the other Army centres of this nature. Stratford has rather more respectable housing in the neighbourhood. Deprivation is perhaps less severe, but problems abound all the same. Some families move every few days to escape debt (including rent) collectors while the two goodwill officers try in various ways to trace them and help them. If the circumstances are rather less dramatic than in Notting Hill, for instance, the overall needs are no less great.

The position in Belfast is somewhat different. The goodwill centre is situated virtually on the border of the sectarian divide. The two women officers are able to assist local homes, giving counsel as well as practical aid. The folk here seem to have accepted the social divisions of Ulster society as a normal part of everyday life. Human nature is remarkably adaptable.

Church-going is much more widespread here than in mainland Britain, especially England. Statistics indicate that over eighty per cent of the population, on both sides of the divide, go to church regularly (apparently that means at least once a month). Spiritual matters are a much more natural part of life, in contrast to the rest of Britain.

The elderly, infirm and inadequate are cared for at the goodwill centre. Children, as well as their mothers, are helped and encouraged in a variety of ways. There are often subtle tensions at home. Sometimes families living near the sectarian border are held hostage by paramilitary groups when they are planning raids across the line. Some families actually 'pay in', in order to remain 'in grace' and thus avoid such unsettling experiences. The centre often becomes a place of refuge. Materially, people are quite well housed; much of the property in the immediate district is quite new. But spiritual and moral needs are always there.

The troubles—a euphemism if ever there was one—may become part of everyday life, but there must be a subconscious awareness of danger all the time. Fear may be suppressed—such is human nature; yet there is a more than average need here for such a haven as the 'Army ladies' provide.

The two women who work from the goodwill centre in the Edge Hill area of Liverpool sometimes find it rather frustrating. The local population, adjacent to the old and rather inadequate Army premises, are mainly of an ethnic minority and another faith. They seem not to appreciate the visits and the offers of help. Major Molly McCormick has never lost her happy Irish nature—or brogue. She simply acknowledges that she and her assistant, Lieutenant Mary Ring, must seek other avenues of approach in their work. Maybe a change of location will be necessary eventually. Their leaders are aware of the problem, and are monitoring the situation. But Molly and Mary don't give up hope. They may sometimes be puzzled, but never in despair; 'knocked down', but 'never knocked out' (2 Cor 4:8–9, Phillips).

If the work in that part of the city is discouraging at present, there are other Army centres where a variety of very useful programmes are conducted. In addition to the three Social Services homes and five corps of varying sizes, there are two places of particular interest here in Merseyside.

The name Childwall Valley could conjure up a picture of a peaceful pastoral landscape—England at its most beautiful. The reality is quite different. Separated from an adjoining middle-class estate by only a railway track, this district knows real deprivation. Up to eighty per cent of school leavers fail to find work. Unemployment overall is well above the regional average. Inevitably that means a lot of young men at a loose end, with temptations from many quarters—mostly criminal. To occupy such fellows, at least keeping them off the streets, seems an important priority.

That kind of work needs special understanding, the ability to mix easily with such youngsters, and a high degree of commitment and faith. The officers presently in charge are

Lieutenant and Mrs Alan Norton—though such designations would never be used locally. The relationship to their lads is very informal; it has to be.

Alan was away on a course when I visited, but his wife, Jo, was well able to enlighten me about this youth and community centre, to use the official term. Her very refreshing Camberwell (London) accent added an element of down-to-earth realism to all she told me.

The little hall, and the quite inadequate patch of ground next to it, are home to anything from fifteen to twenty lads each day, five days a week. Some of them come during the weekends too. They play darts, billiards or pool a good deal, though there are sometimes other activities. The immediate aim is to occupy them until something better turns up. What, how and when are questions to which there are no immediate answers. The local authority provides a grant towards costs and the Army adds its quota. Each of the young lads is expected to pay something, however nominal.

Alan and Jo get to know their 'guests' very well, and have a strong if quiet influence over them. You couldn't brainwash these young men, at least in religious matters, however hard you tried. They just wouldn't come. But there are ways of setting standards and drawing out the best from them. Alan and Jo seem to know instinctively how to do this.

John, aged twenty-five, is unemployed. He has never been able to secure work. But the officer couple, who work as a team, have made him responsible for what goes on. They naturally keep their eyes open, too, though John has proved reliable. Yet responsibility is almost an alien concept to him. He is afraid of it. Never having worked for his living, it is something he is only now beginning to learn—because he has been given a chance. And the other lads, mostly younger, generally respect him.

Leaving the car outside the hall, we asked whether it was safe to do so. Jo's reply was characteristically direct: 'It'll be all right. They know you've come to see us. Otherwise you might find your wheels gone or something like that.' What about their own vehicle? Didn't anyone ever vandalise it? She looked very surprised. 'Of course not. We belong to them, and they wouldn't do anything like that.' It's that kind of district, and these young Salvationists seem to have gained the trust of the local lads.

'Is the hall ever broken into?' I asked.

'Only once, recently,' was the response.

'Much damage?'

'No, just a broken window—oh, and the billiard balls were pinched.'

Of course, that had snookered the activities until a new set was acquired.

'Any idea who did it?'

'Oh yes—but we're not doing anything about it at the moment. He'll take those balls to the second-hand shop down the road, and I've arranged for the man there to let me know when they arrive. The lad wants money, see?'

Such basic understanding and wisdom come only with daily experience, and daily received divine grace and guidance. A few of these young men have come to a genuine conversion experience. Alan and Jo won't rush them, of course. Their backgrounds are not usually the kind of soil in which lush spiritual fruits grow, and there is need for care, spiritual nurture and personal example. But it's an eminently worth-while task. In Jo's words: 'This work is brilliant!'

The boarded-up corner shop premises in the Breckfield district of the city looked as though they might once have served as a local betting shop; I don't know. However, as we got out of the car, the sound of quite tuneful music came from behind those ply-board shutters. My colleague and friend of many years, Major Alan Bennett, said, 'I think we'll both have quite a surprise here. It's my first visit too.' He had recently been appointed as the divisional commander for this part of the country.

The interior looked quite different. In this basically furnished but neat and tidy little hall were eighteen youngsters, ranging in age from about thirteen to twenty-one. Nothing unusual in that, of course. But wait. Each of them had an electronic keyboard, and they were learning to play them.

My enquiries revealed that the neatly-uniformed lady supervising this rehearsal was a retired civil servant who has operated a part-time programme here continuously for the past thirteen years. With short breaks, she has in fact operated this small, but significant community centre for almost thirty years. And the instruments? She has bought them personally, one at a time, as a means of interesting and holding these youngsters (and others before them) through their teen-years.

They are her Sunday school, and she also holds a weekly women's meeting—the Home League. This place was officially closed a long time ago, but Mrs Doris Gibson—officially designated a divisional envoy—was not going to let this little bit of Army influence in a very needy district simply vanish. Unofficial, but with every official encouragement and support, it is a truly sacrificial form of service and influence. From that dark and dingy street corner there is a light which spreads into many of the local homes which she visits to meet and help her ladies and children.

Easterhouse is said to be the largest council estate in Europe. More than 50,000 people live there. Like Drumchapel, the other great housing area in Scotland's largest city, this was constructed to provide decent housing for tenants unable to buy property. Many were transferred from the former slums of Glasgow. One basic omission was the provision of communal facilities for social and recreational activities. That has meant that no sense of community has developed. The area has now been described as a social wilderness and a moral jungle.

Seen from the nearby motorway, the buildings look reasonable. Most of them are conventional terraced housing, with a few semi-detached properties. Some first-time buyers have actually acquired homes here. Prices are lower than elsewhere, I was told, in the hope of attracting people who would stay and help stabilise the community. But as Aux-Captain Eric Buchanan told me, 'Nobody in his right mind wants to live here now.' Buchanan and his wife, Anne, had been there for four years when I met them. This widely-travelled Cockney—he was in the Korean War, and later lived in the USA—fits into the pattern of need here in a way few could do. Their very modest little apartment is above the two halls—one for meetings, a kind of chapel, and the other for various gatherings. Although it is their home, it is in fact open house to lots of people—though most folk are seen, counselled and given practical help downstairs. When they come it is always, 'A cuppa?'—for tea is constantly available in the tiniest of kitchens.

Buchanan is known to most people in his district within the overall area. Driving around in the well-marked Army minibus, he greets individuals and groups by name. 'Hello, George; seen Tom lately? Is he drunk again?' Or, 'Coming Tuesday? You're not? Why not?' and so on. He stops to chat, to enquire about those he is concerned for, and sometimes to challenge: 'What yer got there?' to a lad, as he hastily hides something behind his back. A pertinent question or two reveals that the boy 'found' the radio-cassette player (brand new). 'Fell off the back of a truck, then?' he teases, as the lad now tries to sell him the 'acquired' article. 'Won't do yer no good, pinching things. I'll come round and see you.' And he goes on his way. 'So many of these youngsters get into crime. They've nothing else to do.'

He knows so much about those who live nearby. 'See that little girl? She looks about ten, but I tell you she's thirteen—and she's on the game [prostitution] around here.' Childhood, with its innocence passed her by—and many others like her brought up in this atmosphere.

An hour or two with Buchanan, cruising around the neighbourhood, included two or three house visits. I thought I had seen deprivation and squalor, but here was a new dimension. One of the problems many suffer from is debt. Lack of any kind of budgeting, spending on non-essentials and other forms of inadequate house-keeping are only part of the story. When money is borrowed, loan sharks—who charge the poorest folk astronomical (and illegal) rates of interest to help them buy a cooker or washing machine—are adept at escaping detection by the law. They use 'strong arm' men to extort their 'dues', and are not above breaking in to repossess the gadget if there is no answer to their knock. Physical assault is an everyday occurrence, and many people experience great fear—yet do not know how to avoid falling into the clutches of such criminals.

Those who know the residents say that most are on drugs, and alcohol helps people to forget their troubles. Gang warfare (conducted on what pass for football pitches), marital disputes, family quarrels and fights, drug-pushing with all its attendant evils are all part and parcel of life here. What can be done to help change the situation?

Bob Holman is a former university lecturer who now works for the National Children's Homes—in Easterhouse. He actually lives there, and has researched the situation in considerable depth. He has also worked closely with the Buchanans. He writes about the moral morass and personal distress he has discovered, in the national press (usually the *Guardian*) and for certain professional journals. One of his articles relates the story of a local family who have become Christians through the Army's ministry there. Arthur Colley suffered the agonies of withdrawal after years of alcohol and drug abuse, but is now converted, as is his wife. They talked to me a little about themselves. But Holman knows much more of this radical transformation, as Arthur now works under his direction—right there where he has spent virtually all his life, and where so many know him.

That takes special courage, which he finds in divine grace, day by day.

The Buchanans say, very simply, 'People need to be loved'—and they are by no means sentimental people! They try at least to build up trust and confidence in a place where such qualities are at a premium. That way people will gradually open up and reveal their true feelings and deeper needs. The Captain can get clothing, and maybe a few second-hand refrigerators or washing machines, for those who need them to make a start. But it is in tackling spiritual needs that their true work lies. His account of family situations as he has discovered them indicates all too clearly the need and hunger for moral and spiritual uplift.

A mother, with ten children by a variety of fathers, has a stream of men visitors to her home. It's one way to help earn enough to feed and clothe the family. The eldest is a girl of seventeen, who desperately needed to be taken out of that kind of environment. The Buchanans arranged for her to move into a flat of her own—hopefully out of moral danger. There is always the fear that she will end up following her mother's example—but while they have any influence, they will try to use it.

One practical way of helping at least a few of the army of unemployed is to give them something to do. In collaboration with Aux-Captain Buchanan, the Army's Community Services Officer for Scotland, Major Paul Latham, organised a small work group of able-bodied men. They became known locally as 'the garden party'—though any resemblance to the guests at Holyrood Palace or elsewhere is remote, to say the least. Supplied with protective clothing, free travel and meals, each man received a modest cash payment for each day's work. This consisted of improving the grounds of several Social Services centres in the region, and upgrading a number of Army halls. Several hundred trees were planted on Army premises, with all costs being met from the movement's own resources. Buchanan gave

day-to-day supervision while Latham, a graduate agricul-
turalist, directed operations. It was a small and tentative
beginning, but the experience gained was as valuable as the
service rendered. It is hoped to renew and extend the idea,
for by such means men without work acquire a sense of
personal worth and human dignity in contributing to
communal development. And it keeps them from far less
useful and helpful pursuits.

* * *

If the foregoing account has concentrated on just a few of the
several hundred Salvation Army centres with a community
outreach, it is not for want of appreciation for what is being
done elsewhere. The main intention has been to highlight in
some detail the serious and widespread problems which
exist in very many communities up and down this land—
problems which call for urgent and compassionate action.
Many of the situations and incidents could be repeated over
and over again elsewhere. A common pattern of need can be
discerned. A highly motivated movement is ready to act in
response to these needs, almost anywhere and at any time.

I want to summarise some of the many initiatives and
innovative programmes undertaken by Salvationists across
the country. It must again be emphasised that they operate
alongside scores of other groups, most of which focus upon
one particular need or problem. One home counties newspaper alone publishes a weekly list of over eighty such
facilities. Perhaps one of the Salvation Army's greatest
advantages is its network of established centres—there are
just over a thousand of them in Britain—and the nationwide
co-ordination of its personnel.

Reference was made in Chapter 3 to a number of the
programmes which relate to families operated by individual
Salvation Army corps. Most of them are a form of outreach
into the local communities. Notable among these is the
League of Mercy. Almost 400 such groups exist, with a total
membership of nearly 3,000 volunteers. To single out one

particular unit may seem invidious, yet the Army's own press has given considerable publicity to the operation in the Staple Hill area of Bristol. Under the leadership of David James, an administrator in a local hospital, the group has extended its influence in the district. Systematic visitation of local hospitals, residential homes and institutions is made, not forgetting the housebound, lonely and handicapped in their own homes. Shopping, cooking, gardening and decorating may be undertaken where necessary. Letters are written, sympathy and counselling offered to the bereaved, and food, clothing and furniture supplied in emergency situations.

'The League of Mercy puts love in touch with need,' wrote the editor of the weekly *Salvationist*. All the groups established for this purpose are engaged in at least some of the above expressions of practical concern, reflecting God's love for all.

In the very heart of that same city, in an area which has become notorious for prostitution, racial tensions and other major social problems, stands the Army's Citadel corps. Its new premises, completed very recently, were designed for a considerable expansion of the outreach programme. This operates side by side with the more traditional pattern of Army life, with a good deal of interaction at many points. Under the dynamic leadership of Captain Chick Yuill and his wife, Margaret, the anticipated spread of the corps' influence has already occurred on a considerable scale—which is not to say that there will be no further development.

A Christian pastoral ministry among the prostitutes who ply their trade on the streets has created a measure of trust between them and the Army captains. So much so, that the local police ring from time to time, asking one or other of them to come and accompany a girl home after she has been in court—especially if it was her first appearance. There is already evidence of a change of heart and of lifestyle in two or three of these young women. A fifteen-strong team of counsellors from local churches are assisting in this work, following a police operation—code-named 'Accost'—on street crime. A Sunday meal for vagrants, squatters, punks and others brings together as motley a group as can be found in any place of worship. Yet this has proved to be yet another means to an end. Those receiving food are known, and are deemed to need it. Far beyond that, however, the Salvationists perceive a much deeper and greater need—and endeavour to meet it. Like the apostle Paul, they seek to be 'all things to all men', striving 'that by all possible means [they] might save some' (1 Cor 9:22).

At Hemel Hempstead, north-west of London, a Monday afternoon Carers Club meets. This offers an opportunity for those whose responsibilities include the ongoing and very demanding care of relatives or friends who are handicapped or seriously ill. A burden shared is a burden halved for these people.

The Moorcroft Sunday Club, organised by Salvationists in Hillingdon, West London, has been prominently featured in the *War Cry*. About seventy-five mentally handicapped people meet here every Sunday afternoon, and seem to have the time of their lives. The physical and mental stimulation of various recreational and creative activities, as well as discussion periods and cultural occasions, does wonders for such folk. Enormous energy and patience are needed, but the possibilities are boundless. Gwen White, the organiser, and her helpers—all volunteers—prove that God's limitless grace is available to them. Their joy is to see what it means to these, some of God's most precious children.

A number of traditional Salvation Army corps have now developed community centres, parallel to the more conventional programmes. Wood Green, in north London, has almost seventy volunteers, most of whom work there part time in one or other of the various activities: coffee mornings, with the chance of a friendly chat, a luncheon club, a creche, a weekly get–together for young mums and their smaller children, and so on. Only two or three of the staff are there on a paid basis.

Brigitte Sheppard, who has never quite lost her German accent, is seen by many as a real 'angel of mercy'. Very down to earth in her approach to human needs, she has come to know a considerable number of the most needy residents of the Borough of Haringey. The local authority social workers refer many people to the Army—and Brigitte is there.

Some of the young local Salvationists help her in cleaning out houses which sometimes look like rubbish tips. They move furniture, lay lino and undertake other similar tasks. Brigitte also makes home visits to dozens of people living within a radius of several miles. In so doing she has helped restore many of them to a relatively decent and hygienic standard of living. Above all, her ministry has revived hope in them.

The West Hunslet corps in Leeds has a wide agenda of communal involvement. The hall is very close to a particularly deprived area of the city. Individual soldiers of the corps, bandsmen and others, use their personal skills and resources to help extend the hand of friendship and care to their near neighbours, some of whom need it so desperately.

In the central part of Glasgow there is the Army's City Centre, catering for extreme need among homeless and often helpless people. A number are immigrants who live in appallingly cramped and unsanitary conditions, sometimes paying exorbitant rents to unscrupulous landlords. There is a latch–key programme for children whose parents have to go out to work before school in the morning, returning sometime after the end of classes. Nearby, in the Laurieston district, Captain and Mrs David Arnott exercise a special ministry to around 100 vagrants, mostly alcoholics. Operating just opposite the local police station, they are available seven days a week. Meals are supplied, a soup run goes out most nights to the individual pitches where men sleep out, and above all practical help is offered in Christian love.

A scheme is being developed in a central part of Edinburgh for AIDS victims, their families and concerned friends. Local authority personnel and city hospital staff are co-operating in this project. It is difficult for most of us to realise the degree of anxiety and fear experienced by the spouses of people diagnosed as HIV positive. 'Have I got AIDS too? Will the children get it?' The aim of this projected counselling and referral centre is to help relieve such deep worries by professional advice and tests undertaken at local medical centres. All this is to be in total confidentiality with the back-up of Christian love and understanding.

A similar project is already operating several hours a week at the Wandsworth, South London, corps. A community lounge, the Oasis, is available for a period each Saturday, and the hope is to extend this facility. The target group is similar to that involved in the Edinburgh scheme, and here in inner London the programme operates on a self-support basis. Perhaps no one can understand the fears of those involved like people who are in the same boat. There is clearly a great need to extend help to more of those caught up in this menacing modern phenomenon.

In Manchester, local Salvationists have embarked upon the 'Reach out for Kids' project. A canal boat is presently (August 1989) under construction, to be used on the regional network of waterways—eventually even further afield. Whole groups of children from deprived backgrounds, or up to four one-parent families, can be offered a holiday afloat. The principal target areas are Old Trafford, Sale and Altrincham.

Included in the plans are training for selected older young people, giving them responsibility for such groups. In this way they will be helped to develop their leadership potential. Low self-esteem among many of these youngsters is very prevalent, and this kind of support and encouragement can transform their lives, given the will to succeed.

In Northern Ireland, a rapidly expanding Army programme in Lisburn is being financed through the operation of two charity shops run by the local corps. A number of ACE (Ulster equivalent of YTS) trainees, together with their supervisors, are involved in these activities.

In Portadown, the local Army corps operates The Haven. This programme is designed to help drifters and others without work, aims or hope, as well as their families. Premises at the rear of the corps meeting hall are open, and the men concerned come there from around nine in the morning until four in the afternoon each day. Their wives are visited at home, where some almost unbelievable situations have been discovered. When the husband spends all he receives from the DSS on cheap wine or other alcoholic drink, the family inevitably suffers. In trying to help alleviate such distress, Captain Andrew McCombe and his helpers work in close co-operation with the local authority social welfare workers, and with the police.

Occult practice is quite widespread, and this is a very difficult matter for Christians. The true nature and extent of occult activities is usually shrouded in secrecy, but the believer's faith in the power of God as being greater than all evil forces has to be the foundation of his stand. The reality of the struggle between good and evil is emphasised in Paul's exhortation to the Christians in Ephesus. Writing of 'the powers of this dark world' and the 'forces of evil' (Eph 6:12), he makes clear that only the 'full armour of God' (v 13) is sufficient to enable God's people to stand their ground on this point.

Certainly Captain Andrew McCombe and his chief assistant, Ron, have proved this through their involvement in some incredible happenings in this otherwise beautiful corner of Ulster. The lure of occultism and Satanism is strong for many people seeking something exciting in life.

Young folk are particularly vulnerable, and they are led, quite subtly, from what they see as harmless practices like the ouija board and tarot cards, into much more sinister activities and surroundings. Some will probably never re-emerge from this shadowy nether-world into normal life.

Salvationists believe that conversion can be experienced by an individual in any of a variety of ways, at any time and anywhere . . . almost. Until I got to Renfrew in South-West Scotland, I had never heard of it happening in a public toilet. But the lady concerned, smiling radiantly, told me in her own broad Scots accent, 'Yes, I got saved in the ladies' loo.' And I had to believe her, because others corroborated the event. Apparently the Army hall was so crowded for one of the many communal activities that this woman and her counsellor (a veteran local Salvationist) had sought a quiet place in the aforementioned convenience. The door was discreetly locked for a few moments while this new Christian committed her life to the Lord. Shyly, and with a little nervous giggle, she added, 'It was all right to kneel down; the floor was spotlessly clean.' It must be true that cleanliness is next to godliness!

Among the many programmes operating here are those catering for the lonely, the frail elderly, the mentally handicapped and victims of strokes or heart attacks. For the latter a weekly clinic is being conducted by a Salvationist from Govan, whose professional training enables her to help the dozen or so people who come regularly to this unpretentious little building. In all, some 200 people find this simple Army hall a place of comfort, healing and encouragement every week. And, as we have noted, some find the deeper peace of salvation in Christ as a consequence of what they experience here under the ministry of Mrs Major Ena Latham.

Other Army centres in this part of Scotland provide similar facilities: Kilmarnock and Barrhead, for instance. Even isolated Rothesay benefits from such a programme. In Kilmarnock a number of young job trainees work out their course at the corps' community centre. Under supervision, they learn what can be done to improve the quality of life for people who are paralysed, for example. There are also fine facilities for the mentally ill or handicapped. As I said at the end of Chapter 4, a day centre for such people has now been established at the Redheugh Centre for adolescents, near Kilbirnie (see p 105). This is one of the more recent initiatives in this particular field.

The example of the Swindon Citadel corps in fitting out a 'dry pub' for those wanting company in a non-alcoholic setting, is being considered by other Army centres. 'The Blind Beggar'—named after the pub in the East End of London outside which William Booth preached as a young man—offers good meals as well as a variety of snacks and soft drinks (I was shown a price list for some seventy varieties of the latter). Originally aimed at young people, this centrally-situated basement now attracts townspeople of all ages. Beyond offering refreshments, this novel programme (it is properly registered as a catering establishment) offers an ambience in which many a spiritual conversation occurs quite spontaneously.

The inner London borough of Hackney is one of the most needy and problematic in the capital. Its population is possibly the most racially mixed in the country. Older Salvationists still think of the former Congress Hall in Clapton as a kind of historical monument within the Army. Only the pillared façade of the old building remains, but 200–300 yards away is a corps building, with its community centre incorporated. Captain and Mrs Fred Thompson are in charge of both. They and some of their colleagues make visits in the neighbourhood. This includes one or two nearby estates well known to the police, and to which various kinds of serious crime are sometimes traced back. Yet the Salvationists are received and feel they have a role to play there.

In other parts of the country Salvationists have developed

schemes in districts of quite distinctive minority ethnic character. Notable among these is the programme overseen by Will Hampton in a part of Leicester with a considerable Asian population. He is the Sergeant-Major within the conventional activities of the Leicester Castle corps. On Sundays he can be found carrying out the duties of that position—the most senior 'local officer' (roughly the equivalent of a deacon) in such a centre. Under his direction, however, the community programme has grown both statistically and in its influence in the district.

Despite the difficulty of working among people of diverse cultures, and of penetrating some of the closely-knit 'communities within communities', folk like Hampton and the Thompsons persevere.

Perhaps the Army's image and aims are rejected, initially at least, by many. Maybe the ways and beliefs of Salvationists are unintelligible or unacceptable to them. Doubtless, the Army has to learn even better how to adapt to such circumstances. But it does believe that the gospel is for the 'whosoever'—thus the attempt to reach out even further into the many and varied communities of Britain today must go on. And it does!

10

In Crisis

Many of the situations related in the preceding chapters are in fact various forms of crisis. The word 'crisis' is actually derived from the Greek language where it means 'decision'— a decisive turning point in life. Any event which creates a new situation, with a definite change of circumstances forced upon someone, can be so described. Crises usually occur suddenly and unexpectedly. In many cases, however, they are the culmination of a process which may have been going on for a considerable time without the people concerned being aware of it.

A simple example would be a young girl who lives promiscuously, until one day she discovers she is pregnant. Or a man who has been engaged for some time in criminal activity, and is then caught—and probably convicted and sentenced to jail. Or someone who continues to over-indulge in alcohol until he suddenly recognises that it's got him in its grip. An astonishing number of these people are apparently caught unawares, and then they and their loved ones are faced with the drama of a crisis situation. Sadly, even the sorry consequences of the first crisis do not deter some folk from reverting to their old ways.

While the number of people unemployed in Britain has been reduced over the past two to three years, there are still very many breadwinners without work. There are far too many youngsters who cannot secure a job when they leave school. When the father of a family is made redundant, generally through no fault of his own, and particularly where new employment is unlikely, it becomes a crisis for the whole family. The total number of jobless represents a national crisis here, as well as in a number of other developed, industrialised nations.

Whole families find themselves in crisis in other circumstances, some of which have been outlined already (see Chapters 3 and 4). Conflict between husband and wife, desertion by one or the other, suspicion of incest by the father (quite often a step-father), serious debt or sudden homelessness for any reason: all these constitute crises for families.

In any crisis like this people need urgent, often immediate help. The concluding chapter of this survey of Salvation Army involvement in bringing some light to darkened corners of British society today, will briefly outline the response of Salvationists to these situations. It will also refer to emergency relief and counselling work when major disasters occur.

★   ★   ★

Much has been written and spoken of our national judicial system, particularly of the severe problems of prisoners and prisons. There is general consensus that our jails are overcrowded, and that in some cases those detained in them suffer inhuman treatment. In particular, such practices as 'slopping out' are roundly (and rightly) condemned.

Judge Stephen Tumin, the Chief Inspector of prisons, reported in early 1989 that more than half the prisoners in this country—around 27,000 in a total population of just over 50,000—'have to use a pot instead of a lavatory. Many have to do so in the presence of one or two other prisoners. The contents may have to remain in the cell for up to eleven hours'.

In reply, the then Home Secretary, Douglas Hurd, could offer nothing better than to announce a scheme whereby 'more than 6,500 cells will get sanitation or access to sanitation *by the end of the century*' (my italics). *The Times*, in a leader dated 21st February, 1989, commented in terms of 'human rights in Britain', and of 'an ordeal for prisoners that is not specified by law, but inherited from an era when the humiliation of prisoners was a routine part of their treatment'.

Small wonder, then, that a former private school headmaster wrote of his 'degradation and humiliation' in jail, where he had been put for sex offences against a girl pupil. Apart from the 'special' attitude of other inmates to such offenders, he was 'appalled by the barbarousness of insanitary conditions, abusive officers and inadequate privacy'.[1]

Whatever the nature of the offences committed, those penned up in the prisons of a civilised nation surely have the right to certain basic forms of decency. Yet these practices persist. Statements are made in parliament about reforming the whole system. There is seemingly endless debate, but progress seems painfully slow. It must seem particularly so for those directly involved.

The whole question of custodial sentences—locking people up for crimes committed—is the subject of long-standing debate. Two hundred years ago Jeremy Bentham was campaigning for reform of the prison system. He even went so far as to declare that 'all punishment is mischief, and in itself evil'. It is hardly surprising that others, no less qualified and experienced as jurists than he, should disagree.

Yet behind his radical comments lies the truth that mere retribution for wrong-doing is virtually useless in raising the standards of behaviour in society. In particular, lengthy isolation from family and community will usually have profound psychological and emotional effects on a person, from which he may never fully recover. The argument that time to reflect on one's misdeeds is important for the rehabilitation of the wrong-doer clearly flies in the face of the facts in most instances. A very disturbing number of men (and some women) go on to commit further breaches of the law and end up in jail again. Some become recidivists, going back inside repeatedly—sometimes for thirty or forty years.

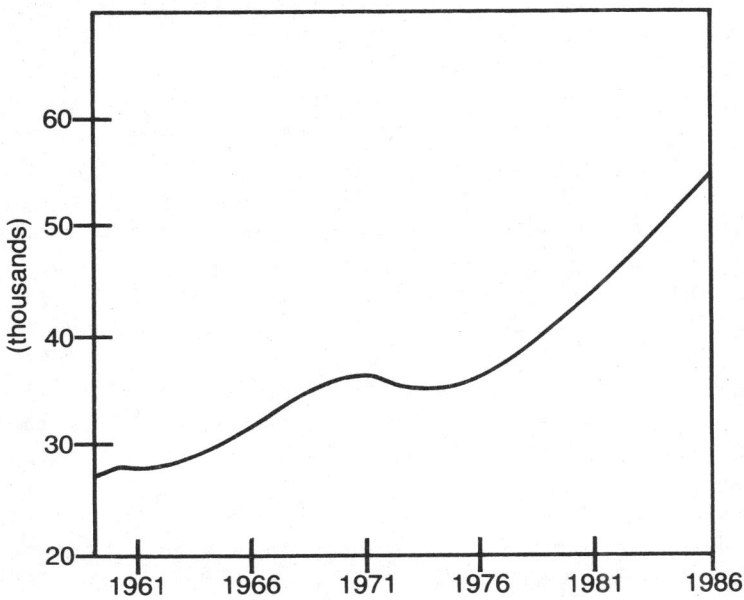

Sentenced prisoners

A number of Salvationists are among those employed in various sectors of the prison service, but so far the Army has not taken any official or active position on penal reform. However, William Booth did not mince his words when writing in 1890 about the conditions prevailing in the country's jails at that time. His comments were, as always, positive and direct:

Our prisons ought to be reforming institutions, which should turn out men better than when they entered their doors. As a matter of fact they are often quite the reverse. . . . On coming out [prisoners] find themselves cursed with the brand of the gaol-bird, far from home, character gone, and with no-one to fall back upon for counsel, or to give them a helping hand.

He went on to write of 'one great qualification for [the Army] dealing with this question'. It was the only religious body 'which has always had some of its members in gaol for conscience's sake', and 'which can boast that many . . . in our ranks have gone through terms of penal servitude'.

The Army's work for prisoners began in Melbourne, Australia, in 1883, and by the following year similar work—at the prison gates—was commenced in London. Individual acts of kindness and compassion in meeting released men as they left the prison premises, and helping them with accommodation, food and eventually work, had undoubtedly occurred even earlier. Only in 1902 was it possible for Salvation Army officers in Britain to visit prisoners who expressed a desire for an interview with them. That work has extended until today there are just on a hundred centres where accredited Army officers or others have regular access. This is co-ordinated nationally within the Prison Chaplaincy Service—though the term needs clarification. The personnel recognised and accepted for this ministry are not official prison chaplains, but rather prison visitors. However, they have a very wide influence, and are able to arrange for liaison with families of inmates, and also for facilities to be made available upon release.

Some prisoners register their religion as 'Salvation Army', usually because of previous residence in a hostel or other social centre. A few have been Salvationists and subsequently fallen foul of the law; they naturally look to the Army representative for a spiritual ministry. Conversions are by no means unknown—there is quite a body of prisoners whose change of heart has led them 'from crisis to Christ'—and that is the ultimate hope and aim of every Salvationist engaged in such work. Incidentally, quite a number of retired Army officers now act as such visitors on a voluntary basis.

Major John Pocock has a remarkable testimony as an ex-prisoner who has since been enabled to help thousands of men and women following completion of their jail terms. I met him and his wife in the living room of their leader's modest home on the outskirts of Manchester. I had heard something of his story, and was grateful for his agreement to some details being included here. They are evidence of what can happen to someone almost born into criminality.

His childhood was difficult and brutal. His alcoholic father was in and out of prison for almost forty years, and eventually remarried a prostitute. Taught by his father to steal, he inevitably found himself in an approved school and then a Borstal (remand) centre. 'I never experienced love or care in any form, anywhere.' And all this in quiet, picturesque Bridgwater, Somerset! Thieving in order to survive, he was finally sentenced to six years in jail. He claims that he was in fact innocent of that offence, but 'I'd done plenty of other things for which I was never caught'. The fact that his father was drunk in court during the trial did not help him.

The local Salvation Army corps officer visited him in the isolation wing, and found a very aggressive inmate—a registered atheist in solitary confinement for violent assault upon a prison officer. 'I only gave him back what he'd given me,' says Pocock now, somewhat laconically. 'I knew no better.'

Brigadier Fensom persevered, however, and on Pocock's release he was met, escorted home for a meal, a bed and, eventually, a job. Rehabilitation was a long and hard process. Conversion was a start, but there was much more to it than that. The young man's lifestyle had virtually excluded any consistent schooling, and the moral and ethical bases which most children imbibe unconsciously from infancy had to be learned from the start. And in a hurry. There were enormous obstacles to be overcome, but he persisted. Since his marriage, his wife has been a great strength to him, he states.

The Pococks have been Army officers now for well over twenty years, all in the Army's Social Services centres. I asked Mrs Pocock how she had come to marry her husband. She laughed. 'None of the other girls [cadets] at the [officer-] training college would even look at him. So I thought, why shouldn't I?' Clearly by this time Pocock had progressed to full membership—soldiership as it is called—in the movement which had given him so much help and encouragement. And it went on from there—and still goes on: this almost unique partnership of Salvation Army officer couples in the tasks to which they are appointed.

As these two special people were leaving the room, Mrs Pocock suddenly said, 'Oh, you didn't show him that.' 'That' was a bundle under his arm, which he had been clutching somewhat tensely during our conversation. It turned out to be a framed 'Certificate of Honorary Fellowship of Manchester Polytechnic'. It had been presented to him when they left the Francis Street Hostel in that city. During the course of the years they had been in charge there—in one of the oldest and most dilapidated buildings the Army maintained, prior to its demolition—he had helped literally hundreds of discharged prisoners on release, mainly from Strangeways Prison. In their confusion, fear and general disorientation, they had found someone who understood their plight. Pocock's own experience had been transformed by the grace of God into an investment of eternal worth and significance. 'For me the most important thing in life is Christ,' he says. And his personal salvation has proved to be a true 'spiritual metamorphosis'. What John Pocock has done in this way can be reflected in what other hostel managers, prison visitors and other concerned Salvationists are doing continually.

It would be false to give the impression that all prisons are inadequate or all staff lacking in compassion. Many penal establishments operate in a humane way, and offer opportunities for self-improvement to those who really want it. Some prisoners secure university degrees or other academic qualifications. Others learn skills which could be of considerable help in their eventual reintegration into society. One such is Roy Tysoe. His story was hinted at in Chapter 3.

The *War Cry* (22nd April, 1989) related the details. Roy has been in prison since late 1977, having been convicted of murder. Filled with remorse at what he had done, he soon made full confession and returned to the Christian faith he had abandoned as a teenager. He began looking for ways of using the years he would spend behind bars in some useful way. He learned to write and transcribe Braille, initially as a means of helping a local school for the blind.

On being transferred from Wormwood Scrubs to a prison in Portsmouth he came into contact with some Salvationists. This soon led him to commence transcribing a collection of Army songs for young people into Braille. Since then he has extended the range of his work to include material distributed by the Salvation Army Association for the Handicapped. Now in an open prison in Gloucestershire, he receives regular visits from one of the Army's prison visitors.

Here again is evidence of what God can do to transform human lives. It is also just one more example of the outworking of the divine pattern of service to those in need: 'I was in prison and you visited me.'

*   *   *

Widespread, long-term unemployment is a serious blight in any country, and governments are desperately anxious to minimise the consequences. The whole of the Western world has seen greatly increased numbers of able-bodied people out of work in recent years. The serious poverty of the nineteenth century was largely the outcome of the Industrial Revolution. Today's situation in the more advanced industrial countries is to a large extent the result of the technological revolution. It is therefore a matter of regret that the fact of such mass unemployment should at times become the subject of acrimonious partisan politicking. No one government can be said to be responsible for the recent state of affairs. The problem is international.

Where individual governments have a very clear duty is in the measures taken to ease the burden upon those directly involved. If these prove to be inadequate, or ineffective, hardship is obviously increased—and there is justification for argument and criticism concerning a government's record. The economic effects upon individuals and families here in Britain, as in most other developed nations, have been considerably modified by the payment of benefits for those out of work. Serious implications still remain for those whose income is suddenly reduced by loss of a job, when they still have financial obligations which will now be difficult, if not impossible, to meet. Mortgage payments are one obvious example. However, this form of state welfare provision at least enables those without work to manage, in most instances.

A more serious effect of persistent unemployment, if less immediately obvious, is the loss of self-esteem and personal worth. This is ultimately true whether the person is one on his own, surrounded by neighbours still employed, or where a high percentage of a local population are affected—though the circumstances clearly vary in certain respects. There will always be some who find useful things to do, and contrive to get by financially. Others may turn to much less worthy pastimes, and slip into crime. A few will simply become very depressed, occasionally to the point of suicide.

Retraining may become necessary where technology determines that the old methods or formerly used materials are no longer relevant or viable. Some whole sectors of industry have been closed down, but it appears that training courses in new skills have often lagged far behind such trends. A variety of attempts by government to meet these needs has been supplemented by schemes devised by progressive firms and some private agencies.

The whole subject is vastly complex, and it would be foolish to attempt here to do more than simply highlight some of the main elements of the situation—particularly as it affects people directly. International finance as well as technological and scientific advances are highly specialised subjects. A more easily understood aspect of the matter concerns the attitudes of those in management, and of the labour force. If those who are caught up in the present tumultuous transformation of industry are not honestly and clearly informed, and wisely guided and advised, suspicion and mistrust will be added to the other negative emotions experienced by the unemployed.

The Salvation Army's response so far has been modest and local. It would far exceed the movement's resources to embark alone upon any major scheme. Nor has the Army felt that such action was indicated. It would be all too easy to over-stretch the limits of personnel available, a possibility which has to be guarded against, while using every opportunity for giving aid for which resources are available.

Prior to the very recent establishment of a combined project in South London, a few individual corps have attempted in small, symbolic ways to help at least a few of the army of the unemployed. Even limited training schemes are very costly, though here and there a pilot project was launched or an *ad hoc* enterprise undertaken. One of the more successful of these was in the Birmingham area, where it is still achieving limited goals. Some twenty trainees are being taught in the Bootle district of Liverpool, and intending care assistants receive training within the employment training programme in Leicester. These latter projects are government-aided.

For several years there have been discussions and negotiations with the local authorities in the London borough of

Southwark about the future of the Army's work in the Spa Road area of Bermondsey. The old hostel buildings were scheduled for replacement, but the site was available for redevelopment, subject to planning permission and appropriate funding. There were differences of opinion about the need for another hostel. Now, however, agreement has been reached and a start made on a training scheme for men and women out of work.

There are many long-term unemployed in this area, but the building construction industry requires more workers with skills in bricklaying, carpentry and decorating. The Employment and Training Division of the construction company J Jarvis and Sons is providing the instructors, the Army land and various on-site facilities, while financing involves the Department of Trade and Industry, the London Docklands Development Corporation and other interested funding groups in the region.

Some 220 places are available each year in a programme lasting about six months—seventy per cent of them for people from the local community. A number of women are included, and will eventually find their way into the building industry. Some of those involved in the project will be undergoing retraining, having previously learned another trade. Plans have been approved for the creation of several local community-based activities, and a Salvation Army officer is available at all times as a counsellor for the participants. Unemployment over a longer period can create deep psychological and domestic problems, as already noted.

While this is not a Salvation Army project, pure and simple, it identifies the Army with the needs and concerns of the unemployed, at least in this area where such help is needed. From this centre a project group will move to the Army's land colony at Hadleigh, Essex, to prepare the way for an extension of the scheme to that area. It is planned that they will be accommodated in caravans for eighteen weeks during the second half of 1989, to undertake this phase of the work. Local people without employment will then receive practical training there—at first with metalwork, carpentry and catering. Again, there is provision for women to participate . . . and not only in catering! The Canvey District Training Association will share in this scheme, with the main funding coming from the Salvation Army. The Catherine Bramwell-Booth Memorial Fund will cover the capital costs of refurbishing the present buildings there, estimated at £200,000. A total of £10,000 raised at the Army's annual Christmas carol service in the Westminster Central Hall in 1988 has been allocated to cover equipment costs.

For many Salvationists and friends, the venue for this latter project will be of special interest. This was the land acquired by William Booth as part of his 'darkest England' scheme, and many thousands of men—referred to as 'colonists'—were prepared here for emigration. It is a happy thought—and by no means coincidental—that one of the great social problems of our times is the focus for yet another attempt by Salvationists to help those in crisis.

*　　*　　*

Thorndale House, situated just off Belfast's Antrim Road, is one of six Salvation Army Social Services homes listed as 'Centres for Families'. In each case that really refers to families which have reached a critical point in relationships, or a breakdown of home life. They need urgent professional help, and are normally referred here by the local authority's social services. The definition of a family can vary from a single young woman with a baby to a couple with several children. In fact, it is seldom that a husband/father comes; he has often been involved in violence towards the family. Others who are received here include single women, which generally implies that they are pregnant. Sometimes women with mental problems are also accepted.

Major Florence Jenkins is in charge of the work in this large and rambling Victorian house. The Army has committed £2m to the construction of a new building adjacent, which will then receive the residents while the present property is demolished to make way for substantial extension to the overall programme.

All this implies that there is as great a need as ever for such crisis therapeutic and rehabilitative work in Ulster—and Salvationists take that need seriously. It also means that Jenkins and her staff have more than enough to keep them fully occupied for as far into the future as anyone can see.

The aims of this place are very much the same as in the other family crisis centres. Emergency accommodation for homeless families, one-parent families and sometimes women on their own, is provided here at Thorndale. All will need supportive care, but with it they are expected to look after themselves and any children. Full families are allocated a large bed-sitting room each, with smaller rooms as necessary for youngsters. Mothers with one or two children have individual rooms.

Every effort is made to create a home-like atmosphere. A variety of activities are included in the programme. Talks on child-care, cooking, flower-arranging and hair-dressing vie for popularity with discussion groups and advice on welfare rights. The importance of corresponding responsibilities is not overlooked either. The staff provide a sensitive and caring environment so that residents can feel safe and accepted.

Residents receive the normal DSS and other allowances, together with any income support or other supplementary benefits. With this they keep themselves, and pay rent for their accommodation. The amounts are agreed with the local offices of the relevant government agencies.

A day-care centre caters for younger children whose mothers go out to work. Older children will attend school and also have access to a games room. A pre-school play group operates each week-day morning under the supervision of qualified assistants. The influence of these surroundings is crucial to their normal development. Jenkins feels that not enough money is invested in sustained influence upon younger children. She believes that if we, as a nation, concentrated for twenty years on baby-to-ten-year-olds, we could transform society.

One of the aims here is to break the cycle of recurring breakdown and relapse of people into crisis. The tendency for disturbed people to perpetuate their weaknesses in their children has already been noted in another context. A classic and horrifying example of this process focuses on Mrs J.

She was, on her own admission, a quite inadequate mother for her three children. This is why she was referred here. While the family was in residence a complex story of incest emerged, involving the father and each of the children. Following his subsequent conviction, efforts were made to resettle this pathetic group, but to no avail.

Further enquiries unearthed the fact that Mrs J's mother had had a record of mental instability. It was therefore not entirely surprising to learn further that her grandfather was also her father. She who was the outcome of an incestuous relationship had lived to see the pattern recur in her own children. But Thorndale House exists, among other things, to care for disturbed people.

It was sheer crisis that brought Mrs M to Belfast from Dublin. She fled following the violent death of her husband, himself a very violent man. Her eldest, a six-year-old daughter, had witnessed the killing. She has needed psychiatric counselling. Each of the children had witnessed their mother receiving physical assault and verbal abuse from their father over a number of years. She now finds emotional and spiritual security at Thorndale, and has the chance to bring up her children in a helpful atmosphere. She has been accepted for rehousing on a priority basis, in the circumstances. For this family, at least, there is light at the end of what has been a very dark tunnel. The crisis is slowly but surely being resolved.

It was something of a surprise to find that the majority of women and their children at Lyncroft House were of Asian origin. This series of inter-connecting buildings in a quiet, tree-lined suburb of Birmingham is another of the Army's crisis centres for families. Women without children are accommodated at The Hawthorns, not far away. I had been led to believe that the main immigrant communities tended to 'care for their own' when in trouble. For that reason, I understood, few such folk are found in any of the Army's centres.

Captain Kathleen Seymour, the officer in charge, confirmed that point, adding that the centres operated by these communities locally were all filled at the time. These ladies were, in fact, a temporary overflow from several of these places. I was left wondering what might lie behind that fact. However, the main focus of my enquiries was the work being done here, as always in Salvation Army centres, irrespective of race, culture or creed.

Up to a dozen mothers, with some thirty children, can be received here at a time. Most of the residents at the time of my visit had been the victims of physical violence, almost invariably by their husbands. The relationship between a married couple from South Asia is very different from the accepted pattern in this country. Young women coming to live here sense the relative freedom of their English counterparts. Their husbands tend to become bewildered and frustrated in such a situation, and sometimes react very violently.

Whatever the racial and cultural background from which people come, basic human nature is much the same. Hence the needs of those taken in by Seymour and her colleagues are all too familiar to those engaged in such work elsewhere.

Most of the women, who usually spend several months in residence, are referred through the local housing department or the police. In the latter case, the housing authority has to become involved at some stage, and certainly when it comes to eventual rehousing. The programme is quite similar to that described for Thorndale House and other places like this. There is also a very pleasant playground at the rear of the premises, where children from the local community (mainly middle-class British people) can play side by side with the youngsters resident at Lyncroft House. The Captain reports: 'The Lyncroft and community children mix and play well together, and it is good to see both sets of mums taking an interest in the activities of their children and the playgroup.'

I listened for some time to Kay, one of the non-Asian minority at the time. (The situation is by no means always as I found it, in terms of racial origin.) She had been referred here with her two children, aged four years and eighteen months, in a state of exhaustion and shock. After months of struggling to keep her marriage intact, and despite bitter treatment from her husband who was often drunk, she finally acknowledged defeat. It had been a case of basic incompatibility from the start, though she claimed to have worked hard to make a go of it. Who is to judge the ins and outs, the rights and wrongs, of such situations? But a young woman with two small kiddies needs a haven when the storms of life batter her into a state of emotional insensibility.

Kay had maintained her work as a nurse in a local hospital to help with the mortgage repayments. In her despair at the worsening domestic situation she had taken an overdose of tablets—probably more a cry for help than a serious attempt at suicide. No one knows how many people, especially women, act similarly when they reach the end of their tether. The final blow came when she discovered that her husband had stolen her cheque book and purse, closed their joint savings account and changed all the outer locks of their home while she was out. On arrival at the centre she was totally confused. 'I just saw a lot of faces, and wanted to die—but I clung to my children.' However, after some weeks of residence, where a large bed-sitting room became home to this little crisis family, she simply said, 'It's all been so much better than I could have expected.'

In the meantime legal proceedings continue for the recovery of her part of the marriage assets. That can be an exhausting, humiliating and deeply frustrating experience: why should she have to go through all this to get what is hers by rights? She is working part time at the hospital, with very understanding and helpful superiors, and has been accepted for rehousing.

A crisis centre is, by its very nature, a place of temporary refuge; somewhere where lives can be reshaped. At Lyncroft House this happens under the guidance and counsel of deeply concerned Christian people working in close collaboration with local government authorities.

Similar supportive programmes and facilities exist in several other cities. Newhaven is a smaller unit in Middlesbrough, able to receive ten mothers and their babies or small children. Young pregnant women, including schoolgirls, are also referred sometimes. The tendency is for residence to be short term, and the aim is to provide support, assessment and training for single (referred to as 'unsupported') mothers with infants considered to be at risk. As in the other crisis centres, individual care is a feature which is generally maintained long after the residents have moved on.

The building, an old-fashioned patrician family house, is not very suitable for this purpose. It is owned by the local authority, with Captain Norma Paget heading a qualified staff. A number of these are Salvationists from the area, and all are Christians—thus providing compassion as well as competence. In each of these centres a brief time is set aside each morning for consideration of spiritual matters. Attendance is optional, but many choose to share in what is seen as a family occasion. Some are certainly hoping to find a genuine solution to their crisis, and the staff are always available for personal conversation along those lines.

Many of the residents have lived in common-law liaisons with a man, who is often the father of the child they now have. In such circumstances the boyfriend is allowed to visit and to share in caring for the child—up to three or four hours a day, usually in the evenings. Overnight stays are not permitted. Basic rules have to be observed, and there is some reserve about some of these young fathers.

Some of the young women (most are still really girls) have come to the centre having left men partners who had assaulted them. In some instances, under advice, legal action is considered. I learned, however, that in virtually all these cases the women withdraw from such proceedings at a certain stage. The attitude seems to be, 'I may need to go back to him if I've got nowhere else to go.' Human emotions are certainly complex!

Each resident's name is put on the council housing list when she first arrives, with a view to eventual resettlement. Here again there is close continual co-operation between the staff and local authority social workers.

Training in baby-care, home economics and other very basic aspects of motherhood is given as an important part of the rehabilitation programme. Amazingly, many of these young mothers have little or no idea how to play with their infants, let alone provide the stimulation so necessary to sound, healthy development. The maternal instinct seems to have been stillborn in them. Regular assessment of a resident's progress is made by the care staff, involving her in the process. That way most of them take the whole matter more seriously than they might otherwise do.

The Mount Cross complex is a much larger Army centre, situated in the Bramley area on the outskirts of Leeds. Opened in 1981, as a joint project by the Salvation Army Social Services and the Salvation Army Housing Association, it stands on the site of an earlier Army social home. The new premises includes twenty-three purpose-built family flatlets in addition to accommodation for eight single women—most with babies. Captain Janice Ley has overall responsibility for the entire programme.

The single mothers participate in a programme similar to that at Newhaven. The flatlets are occupied by families whose circumstances are sometimes truly astonishing. For example, Mrs M lived in South Africa where her husband worked. The marriage foundered, and she returned to Britain with her six children. Being technically homeless, she was referred to Mount Cross.

By correspondence and telephone, she and her husband subsequently agreed to try for reconciliation, but shortly afterwards she was informed that he had been murdered. His employers paid for her to fly out to Johannesburg in order to settle affairs, after which she returned to this country, receiving supportive care and counselling before being re-housed. A second marriage has now proved durable for several years, but she continues to visit those at the centre who helped her so effectively in her hour of need.

The above details are all too brief, and cannot do justice to what is being done twenty-four hours a day, seven days a week, in these crisis centres. Dozens of stories could be related, each confirming the fact of one more individual helped back to stability and relative normality. The work as a whole represents one expression of Jesus' statement: 'Inasmuch as ye have done it unto one of the least of these my brethren, ye have done it unto me' (Mt 25:40, Authorised Version).

★   ★   ★

What about the response of Salvationists to major disasters? These are crises of great drama, often involving heavy loss of life and therefore attracting widespread news coverage. One air crash, for instance, may kill far fewer people than those who lose their lives in road accidents over a given period of time. Yet by its very nature, such an event becomes the focus of national horror, sympathy and—let's be honest—a kind of morbid curiosity. When a hundred or more people die in one moment, it is quite different from the series of tragedies at various points on our road network over weeks or months.

The continual vigilance of the public services is suddenly highlighted too. Hundreds of people involved in police, fire and ambulance services are precipitated into action in an instant. All too often the circumstances in which they then have to operate are intensely harrowing and traumatic. Some even lose their own lives, or suffer serious injury, while attempting to save others. Their names are flashed momentarily onto TV screens and news pages, while rarely a word is said or printed about those who subsequently spend weeks and months recovering from the psychological and emotional effects of such service. It is all part of their dedication. They are trained and equipped for something which will one day explode into their lives unexpectedly, urgently, perhaps even disastrously.

It is a long-established tradition that whenever such an event occurs the 'Sally Ann' will be there with cups of tea, bowls of soup and other sustenance. In the past, liaison with the emergency services in some countries has been even closer and more sophisticated than in this country. To some extent the attitudes of public authorities and even governments have been determinative of the extent to which the Army can respond. Some have applauded sincerely, others more patronisingly. 'There's nothing like an Army cup of tea' is a slogan which seems to limit the kind of help expected of Salvationists to 'a char and a wad' (Cockney for a cup of tea and piece of cake). That expression became familiar to servicemen during World War Two, in particular, as the welcome Red Shield canteens hove into sight. Such material comfort and relief is valid enough. The food and drink offered, often in conditions of considerable physical danger, were very often seen as a form of 'sacrament'. But the kingdom of God does not consist of food and drink—it is spiritual (see Romans 14:17). And man's deepest needs, in any situation, are similarly spiritual. He is created in the image of God—be he a fireman, policeman or doctor.

It follows that in times of extremity, of intense stress and emotional devastation, he may very well need far-reaching spiritual support and counsel. And who better to offer it than the Salvationist, with his strong faith in a God whose grace and strength can be supplied to all, at the times and to the extent that they need it. In this respect, the pattern of Army emergency relief service is changing, though there have always been Salvationists available to comfort the dying or the bereaved when death has struck in such dramatic ways.

As long ago as 1913, a team of twelve Army officers was sent from London to the South Wales colliery of Senghenydd following a major pit disaster. Some 400 men lost their lives, and the whole of this relatively small community was devastated. The Army's Year Book for 1914 records that the group went to stricken homes in twos and threes, where they encountered 'mothers prostrate under the shadow of death . . . unable to attend to their household duties, unable even to prepare food for the clamouring children'. After doing all that was necessary to restore a measure of order in such homes, they 're-inspired the mothers', as much by their timely and practical aid as by their prayers.

In times gone by Salvation Army personnel have acted as unofficial volunteer stretcher-bearers, under fire on battlefields. Today, wherever people gather to wait in desperate anxiety for news of loved ones, or to mourn when that news confirms their worst fears, there is still a great need for someone to be at hand, to listen to sobbed expressions of grief and to put loving arms around stricken fellow men and women. A brief spoken prayer is often profoundly appreciated.

Such spiritual ministry has recently come to be more accepted, indeed welcomed, by the emergency services and social workers. Some professionals still hesitate about 'letting that crowd of do-gooding amateurs in'. One can understand that bungling efforts, however well-intentioned, could create havoc. However, these critics seem unaware that a growing number of Salvationists have had professional and other training in various forms of relief work, including post-disaster counselling. They clearly feel that the 'Sallies' should stick to cups of tea—but by and large there is seen to be a great need for the spiritual ministry, sometimes in near desperation.

At this point it is only right to record that the Army owes a considerable debt to the work of the late Major Joe Burlison. He was both influential and instrumental in the development of the Army's work in this entire field in Britain, over more than two decades.

It would not be appropriate to quote personal incidents associated with recent major disasters in Britain. Sorrow and grief are very private experiences for most of us. If there are occasions when media representatives forget this, we shall not. However, it is of more than passing interest to note the participation of whole teams of Salvation Army personnel in Aberdeen (shore base for operations following the Piper Alpha oil-rig explosion and fire), Lockerbie, the scene of the almost unprecedented form of aircraft sabotage, and the Hillsborough football ground in Sheffield. A group of Salvationists also operated for weeks on both sides of the Channel after the sinking of the 'Herald of Free Enterprise', off Zeebrugge. Other recent major accidents included the crash of an aircraft on the M1 motorway, several rail disasters, and the sinking of the Thames pleasure boat, 'The Marchioness'.

In each case Salvationists were quickly on the scene. They have emergency vehicles, stocked with food, blankets, clothing and other necessary items. There is a well-organised network of contact persons, several of them constantly on 'bleeper' call, to co-ordinate the work. In most parts of the country there are now also carefully negotiated and established arrangements with the public emergency services. In minutes following a serious incident the Salvationists are on their way to the scene.

The four particular disasters referred to above were occasions when a long-term plan of action was commenced to offer spiritual comfort to those most closely concerned. Visits were made to individual homes. Relatives of victims were accompanied to mortuaries, where they had to identify the remains of kith and kin. (One of the most difficult emotional problems concerns relatives where no body can be found. A different approach to counselling then has to be adopted.) In Lockerbie, rather more than elsewhere, counselling of emergency services personnel was maintained for many weeks following the experiences which continued to haunt and torment many of them.

This is a considerable extension of what was formerly undertaken on a spontaneous one-to-one basis. Modern disasters on this scale tend to create much greater havoc, if only because of the larger number of victims and others implicated. The effects of such events are increasingly widespread. Following news of the Pan-Am jet crash in Scotland, American Salvationists were quickly on hand on the other side of the Atlantic, where relatives had assembled for news of their folk. And as stunned Liverpool FC supporters made their way home from Sheffield, Salvationists in their home city were alerted to be available as one family after another was stricken with news of yet another fatal victim at Hillsborough.

The pressures upon those directly involved at hospitals, police stations and other key centres in the wake of such disasters are enormous. Counsellors seeking to comfort and support those severely shocked by their loss face this question: 'What can I possibly do that will mean anything?' The *Way Cry* (20th May, 1989) recorded the reactions of Mrs Captain Ann Holt immediately after the Hillsborough tragedy: 'I didn't pretend to have any answers. There was nothing to say. No glib words. You simply love them. Hug them. Comfort them.' Her husband, Malcolm, later added: 'I shall never be the same again'—and that is the reaction of thousands who experience those pressures, that moral burden. Days and nights on end, they take their toll. The counsellors themselves need to recharge their emotional and spiritual batteries. They have to find release from the loads which have shifted onto them in the course of their ministry.

Professionals refer to a 'de-briefing', which is rather a cold and clinical term. The word 'off-loading' is much more expressive of the true cost of such involvement. Mrs Major Mary Elvin shared with me her experience. Having been one of the first on the spot after the tragedy at Lockerbie, she and a younger colleague continued to visit the village week after week. They were trying to help some of those most deeply affected by all that they had seen, heard and sensed on that night. Many were firemen.

She described her own needs: 'I just knew I had to off-load. I couldn't have gone on receiving all that those poor men were putting onto me without something of that kind.' At the time of our conversation, months after the event, she went to such a session after each visit to the site of the disaster. Another officer also trained in counselling was able to ease Mary's burden, thus enabling her to continue to fulfil her role.

What she has done and felt, together with Ann and Malcolm Holt and many other fellow-Salvationists, on such macro-occasions, is reflected on a smaller scale in the scores of lesser emergencies to which the Army's emergency vehicles and volunteer workers are called. In material terms, the provision of food, clothing and shelter is simply a response to people's material needs, about which our heavenly Father knows (see Matthew 6:31–32). The task of 'weeping with those who weep' is part of the Lord's own ministry, which his servants are privileged to share. He was anointed—set apart—to heal the broken-hearted and share the good news, even in such starkly tragic circumstances, that God loves; he cares; he heals. That is the over-riding motivation of Salvationists who, together with so many others, get their hands dirty in identifying themselves with the extremities of human experience.

Note

1. Michael Bettsworth, *Marking Time* (MacMillan: London, 1989). Reviewed by Catherine Bennett in *The Times* (10th February, 1989).

Conclusion

In one sense there can be no conclusion to the type of work described in the previous pages. The needs are there, as they were in William Booth's day—and long before that. They will certainly still be there for the foreseeable future. Hence this record is of necessity incomplete. Apart from the continuing nature of the work, much that is currently being done by Salvationists is missing from this book. The centres of work referred to are only a limited selection from the total of Salvation Army undertakings in Britain today. The inclusion of stories related to particular homes and other social centres does not imply that those places operate more effectively than others—far from it! These are simply sample glimpses into the widespread ministry of this movement—today's inheritors of Booth's compassion, vision and enterprise.

The Salvation Army's relatively brief history as a part of the church universal has seen some significant changes in the efforts made by its members to meet the deeper needs within society. Many improvements in the overall provisions for ameliorating the distress and misery of the poor and disadvantaged are recorded here. Yet many of my colleagues involved in these endeavours say, quite simply, 'Basically, little if anything has changed in the past hundred years.'

They imply that the 'submerged tenth' persists, for one reason or another, and that something still has to be done to uplift that segment of our population.

It is an on-going process, and will continue to attract Christians who are sensitive to the whole biblical ethos and its implications. God created all mankind equal in terms of moral and spiritual worth—however much individuals may differ in their capacity to achieve and create. Christ died for all. Hence a concern for both the temporal and spiritual welfare of all must find expression in practical deeds. And that must apply particularly to the genuinely under-privileged, handicapped or gravely sinned against. It must also be extended to those whose deprivation or degradation are of their own making, the outcome of their own folly and fecklessness. God does not give up on such people; neither can we as disciples of Christ.

As to whether the programmes undertaken by Salvation-ists and others are the best that could be devised must remain a matter of judgement, under divine guidance with the hindsight of experience. That, too, is a continuing process. Indeed, one of the difficulties encountered in compiling this record has been the continually changing scene over a period of months, and long before publication. New pro-grammes are constantly under consideration. The London homelessness survey referred to in Chapter 5 is an example. Research will continue even after this book appears; thus the story is as yet unfinished. Personnel changes occur from time to time, and some whose stories are included here will have moved on to other work by the time these pages are read.

Changes in government legislation, particularly in DSS provisions and conditions, continue apace. The very names of certain benefits have been altered—as well as the criteria on which they are based—to the considerable confusion of many for whom they are intended. Government policies, too, are subject to revision—and sometimes to considerable delays. The long-awaited reply to the report prepared by Sir Roy Griffiths on care in the community for residents discharged from long-stay institutions is a case in point. A parliamentary response is awaited as these lines are being written. Political reactions to some such reports and enquiries may take several years. In the meantime, the debates in parliament, as well as around the country, continue. Some of them are well-prepared and highly significant. Others appear to be attempts to score partisan points, or to procrastinate on (if not actually to set aside) 'delicate' issues in terms of attracting votes.

It has never been the policy of the Salvation Army to engage in outright attacks upon any government. William Booth did not do so, and his successors have not felt that this was the way for them, at least, to register their deep concerns about government policies. Representations are made to government departments and ministers, irrespective of which party may be in power at the time. Honest, well-documented lobbying is another means of bringing pressure to bear upon the nation's legislators, where the Army's experience indicates that changes in the law are necessary. References to such action are made at several points in this book.

Thus the summary of 'Matters for Concern' which follows, represents the working experience and convictions of Salvationists actually on the job. In this connection, I have consulted closely with colleagues who know better than I what is happening, and what ought to be done to enhance the care of several million of the poor and needy of many types in our land. In that sense, the concerns expressed and the challenges issued come from the Army, collectively.

As mentioned earlier, the work of the Salvation Army is conducted alongside, and often in close collaboration with, other agencies and associations. A considerable number of these are just as dedicated in their Christian motivation as the

Salvationists. Some are even more highly specialised in certain fields: work among children, for example, or for the handicapped. Others have a longer history of such work than the Army. There are also the professionals—even if for some of them the moral and spiritual dimensions are not always present in their approach to their work.

The Salvation Army may justly claim to have pioneered quite a number of rescue, rehabilitation and general relief programmes. The subsequent development of such work, however, has been advanced by and enriched through co-operation with at least some of these workers. There is no claim to exclusivity in the thinking of Salvationists, though the variety of its undertakings may be unique in any one registered charity or section of the church.

The ultimate goal of all Salvation Army work is spiritual—saving souls, as most of its members think of it. They believe that only through regeneration and transformation of the whole person, by the Spirit of God, can true and lasting rehabilitation be accomplished.

Their motivation is true and sure. Their determination to serve the needs of their fellow men and women in need is tempered only by the awareness of their own need of divine grace and compassion. Given the tremendous and continuing needs in Britain, these present-day servants of Christ might paraphrase the words of their founder in his last public address:

> While one family is tragically torn apart by
> bitterness or indifference, or through love turned
> to hatred — We'll fight!
> While one child is denied its human dignity,
> through physical, sexual or emotional abuse — We'll fight!
> While one bewildered adolescent loses his way
> early in life, through bad example, or lack
> of love or discipline — We'll fight!
> While one elderly person is unloved, unwanted
> or uncared for — We'll fight!

While one homeless man or woman has to sleep
   rough, or bed down in a derelict house or
   a vermin–infested shelter   —   We'll fight!
While one despairing alcoholic, or misguided
   drug-abuser staggers towards self-destruction —   We'll fight!
While men go in and out of prison, and women
   go in and out of abortion clinics   —   We'll fight!
While millions of our fellow countrymen in
   Britain wander in spiritual darkness, and
   in ignorance of God's love   —   We'll fight. . .
                                            to the very end!

Matters for Concern

This list represents some of the major concerns felt by the Salvation Army: its leaders and workers. The 'success' ethos of much present government thinking and action appears to conflict with biblical teaching. Responsibility for one's neighbour, with compassion and practical aid for the despised and the outcast, the weak and the inadequate, is very clearly enjoined in the Scriptures.

Salvationists engaged in this ministry often note with dismay and sorrow the growing polarisation of society in terms of material acquisition. The pursuit of success tends to produce in many a selfish preoccupation with personal advancement. Where this occurs at the expense of their less fortunate, capable or successful fellow citizens, it must give rise to real concern.

The summary which follows covers most of the subjects dealt with in this book. It also represents virtually the whole spectrum of national life. We hope that it will alert the reader, as well as challenge all public authorities with responsibilities in their areas. It will no doubt act as a strong stimulus to our own policy-makers, and to all who work in the spirit of compassion as their response to God's love for all mankind.

The Salvation Army is concerned about:

1. All that threatens family life, the stability of marriage and the ability of parents to create secure, loving homes for their children. This includes:
   (a) The emotional trauma of parents contemplating or instituting divorce proceedings.
   (b) The effects of marital discord and conflict upon any children of the marriage.
   (c) The long-term emotional consequences of child abuse in any form.
   (d) The vulnerability of children and young adolescents coming out of care, or leaving home under stress—drifting all too often into homelessness.

The present divorce legislation needs considerable strengthening, particularly by ensuring a period of serious reflection before legal proceedings are embarked upon. More adequate counselling facilities are required, with a stronger obligation on both parties to submit to a process aimed at reconciliation—or at least of conciliation. This would naturally imply greater government financing.

Submissions by the Salvation Army, as well as by many other concerned groups, have detailed a number of ways in which the legal basis of divorce could be amended so as to help stabilise marriage and family life.

2. All that tends to reduce the quality of life of the elderly. To this end, there must be:
   (a) A greater recognition of their intrinsic value as people, and their potential for continuance in some form of useful contribution to society.
   (b) More adequate provision of all necessary services for the dependent elderly and their carers.

The implementation of those parts of the Griffiths Report which the government has accepted in principle so far, must include proper central government funding to enable local authorities to carry out adequately their considerably broadened responsibilities under the proposals. This applies to both residential and domiciliary care of the elderly—and also to the situation of the mentally ill. Without such funding many authorities would find it impossible to establish and maintain the programmes envisaged.

3. The unacceptably high incidence of homelessness. Some of the causes have been outlined in the previous pages, but the Army's concern includes:

(a) The present serious lack of housing at affordable rents, or prices, as a result of political decisions and policies. Where the almost impossibly high costs of housing are the consequences of allowing market forces to determine prices, such policies will inevitably exclude very many from being decently housed. This is not only wrong, but ultimately immoral. Reasonable housing is the right of every citizen. The present low levels of wages, combined with very high rents, or mortgages, serve to deny several million people in this country that right.

(b) The need for more flexibility in providing for the homeless, including direct access and emergency procedures, with sensitive attention to special needs.

(c) The urgent need to ensure adequate primary health care for the homeless. Many suffer quite needlessly for lack of such provision.

Funding is necessary for the 'care' component in the programmes of the Army's (and similar) hostels. They are not merely 'dosshouses' providing solely emergency accommodation. Caring for the whole person, body, mind and spirit, is an integral part of Salvation Army philosophy—but this does not come cheaply. Professional staff are required to help residents suffering from the stress and mental anxiety of modern life.

Further, the separation of the 'housing' and 'income support' elements in the proposed new funding system creates a most unenviable task for those directly involved in the management of these centres, however convenient it may be in terms of government accounting.

4. All that contributes to material poverty in any of its forms. This includes:

   (a) The almost uncontrolled personal credit system in this country at present, which encourages many to spend far more than they can afford. The number of credit cards in circulation is much greater than in the major industrialised European nations. The need for tighter credit control, at this level at least, seems self-evident.

   (b) The virtually inescapable spiral of repayments, with interest, for those who incur such debts. For many this creates feelings of sheer despair, as they sense themselves hopelessly enmeshed. There is particular need to do more to counter the nefarious practices of the 'loan-sharks' with their scandalously high rates of interest.

   (c) The introduction of the Social Fund loan system has not solved the problem of those who need emergency one-off payments to help them emerge from a temporary plight. Many agencies, including the Salvation Army, now receive a growing number of requests for financial assistance from people who would formerly have received a grant. Loans tend to perpetuate indebtedness for those at the bottom of the economic ladder.

5. The desperate need to improve the appalling conditions in many prisons today, as rapidly as possible. Beyond this is the continuing call for a radical review and ultimate reform of the whole penal system. This will require careful study of alternatives to imprisonment for less serious offences. A number of other countries have highly developed systems of such non-custodial forms of sentence as community service.

   The situation would be transformed once the overcrowding of prisons was substantially reduced. To this end, the Salvation Army urges the government to enter into intensive, high-level consultation with voluntary bodies working in this field. Particular issues highlighted by the Army's official prison visitors include:

(a) The need for a vastly improved remedial and rehabilitative programme, to avoid the destructive and hugely expensive cycle in which prisoners often emerge with stronger criminal tendencies than at the time of their incarceration—often re-offending very soon after release.

(b) The need for a more developed aftercare service following release. The shock of readjustment to society, and the temptation to return to the criminal fraternity are very great, and far too many succumb. The Salvation Army Social Services are giving careful attention to the possibility of extending the support facilities needed by prisoners at this stage. It is recognised that most are quite disorientated after long periods shut away from the realities of society and its constant evolution. Help for the families concerned is also needed particularly at these times.

6. The particular problems of inner-city populations.

Much has been said and written on this complex subject, and a great deal has been accomplished in some cities. Plans are well advanced for the economic regeneration of more such places, and this will undoubtedly have positive social repercussions. However, the greater part of today's 'submerged tenth' is still to be found in these communities; poverty and squalor, degradation and vice still abound, as recorded in several chapters of this book. More permanent solutions to these problems seem as far off as ever.

In the face of such stark realities, the Salvation Army pledges itself to continue, and where possible intensify, its close-up ministry to those blighted by the conditions prevailing in many deprived and run-down urban areas. It urges all concerned, including national and local authorities, churches and a range of voluntary agencies, to do their utmost to ensure more adequate standards of living for such people. Housing and health, employment and recreation, as well as education and appropriate cultural facilities, are priority matters. Only in this way, with large-scale financial input over a longer period of time, can the quality of life in these areas be significantly improved.

7. The needs of certain particularly vulnerable categories of people in the community. These include:

(a) The mentally ill, for whom more care is urgently needed. Many are released from psychiatric hospitals and similar institutions without any assurance of follow-up attention. Others leave families, homes and jobs because of their condition. They are generally incapable of caring properly for themselves. More community facilities must be provided, particularly to ensure that essential medical attention is received; such people will not usually take any initiative to seek this. However, given care a good number who suffer from any form of mental illness are capable of surprising levels of achievement.

The Salvation Army deeply regrets the rejection by the House of Commons of the Schizophrenia Aftercare Bill, following the welcome given to its provisions by the House of Lords.

(b) Others who are damaged in one way or another— physically, mentally, emotionally or spiritually. The need for well-run residential centres for these people should be re-evaluated. This would include places for endangered children and disturbed adolescents (see point 1 above), the mentally ill (see point 7 above) and alcoholics who are seriously affected by their condition.

(c) Those with alcohol and drug-related problems. The widespread availability of alcohol, and its general social acceptability, belie the grave consequences of excessive consumption. What many regard as a safe level for them very easily escalates to create physical and psychological dependence.

Based on its worldwide experience in helping such people for more than a century, the Salvation Army will continue to exert pressure on the government to reduce the availability of alcohol by:

(i) controlling the number of outlets, as well as licensing hours;

(ii) increasing the price by levying duty at higher rates (both these means have proved effective in a number of other countries);

(iii) controlling advertising; and above all

(iv) stepping up education to counter the image of alcohol consumption as desirable or even necessary.

We are resolved to help promote such education, with a view to emphasising the reasonableness of total abstinence, and to encourage an alcohol–free lifestyle.

Constrained by the love of God, and in compassion towards so many of our fellow men and women, we offer this resume of major social and moral needs. We commend this expression of our concerns to the careful study, and prayerful consideration of all readers. We firmly believe that the recommendations made are in accord with the overall will of God for those whose potential for positive and creative development is stunted by the problems recorded here.

Index

God's Grey Warriors

by Michael Apichella

Today we are witnessing the greying of the West. More and more people are living beyond the age of sixty-five, releasing rich resources as well as creating complex problems.

Drawing on Scripture and the examples of contemporary Christians, Michael Apichella shows that the elderly have a wealth of experience, gifts, wisdom and time to offer in practical and pastoral ways. Administration, evangelism, prayer, counselling, visitation and caring for children are just a few of the many areas he considers.

Realistic and compassionate, the author does not evade the problems afflicting the elderly. He also gives disturbing evidence of the West's deep-rooted prejudice against old people, discussing the underlying causes of the malaise.

'Michael Apichella's book comes as a welcome reminder of the potential that is sitting in our pews. There are few books which tackle the problems and opportunities of the "grey" economy and fewer still which provide such a thorough exploration of the subject.'
—JOHN WHEATLEY in his Foreword.

Monarch
Publications

Born To Shop

by Mike Starkey

'A witty, penetrating analysis of the consumer society.'
  —**TIM COOPER,** former co-chair, The Green Party

The West has become a massive shopping arcade, a world of slick marketing images selling us everything from toothpaste to prime ministers.

Born To Shop is a humerous and provocative romp through our throw-away culture, its fads, fashions and personalities. Mike Starkey celebrates the fun of consumption, but warns of the dangers if it dominates other values. He illustrates the sacrifices of relationships and environment, and the lives wrecked by debt as we relentlessly pursue the Good Life.

He challenges our personal and national priorities and points to a refreshing alternative not based on disposable goods and gaudy packaging.

MIKE STARKEY is a broadcaster, journalist and poet, currently working as a reporter in commercial radio. As Press Officer at the Jubilee Centre he was in the forefront of major campaigns on consumer debt and Sunday trading. He is author of *Frogs And Princes,* a hilarious collection of verse. He regularly performs on TV and radio.

Monarch
Publications